Letters from Amalfi
An American Abroad

J. R. Johnson

Author's Note

The best way to describe the coast is to share with one how one feels when one leaves the coast. That's the miracle moment when you know that you will be returning. When a place moves you, when you already miss the scents of summer on the breeze, the boats making their constant treks between Positano and Amalfi and racing to Capri with the hulls full of tourists on their own paths of discovery, and the tastes that linger on the palate. But perhaps it is the people of the coast that resonate most in one's mind as you round the corner in Positano at *Bar Internazionale*[1] that you realize that it is all about to be behind you, and you begin to tear – just a little – but that tear says it all. Then, I know, you will return.

---

[1] *Bar Internazionale.* Its location at the promontory – along a curve in the only road between Sorrento and Salerno – allows it to serve as the gatekeeper to the coast. For those coming or going by cycle, car, or bus on the road or on foot, trekking to or from *Il Sentiero degli Dei* (Path of the Gods) above, all paths pass passed this bar – it is the first and the last landmark one sees when coming or going.

Dedication

A dedication—the final piece to scribe to you... just for now... I really must first thank the ladies—those pillars of my world, then and now, those women that helped make every page possible...

... So, to my three Muses... Jackie Chan, Claudia, and the most stellar setting sun—as only seen from our side of the mountain... and, if not for Giuliana and her tales of better homemaking... and Caterina, our idol from Toscana—without, none of this would have ever occurred...

... To Marlise Senzamici, for those initial two years of taking my notes and scribes from journals and scraps of paper to this... Thank you for your patience and guidance... and, lastly, to Monie, for your true dedication to my vision and our countless hours of reliving every one of them...

... And to the Gentleman...

To Giulio, for opening my eyes to the real costierra... and to dear Stefano... Thank you for teaching me the real meaning of "piano, piano..." And to our patron saint, Generoso... who was then, and will always be just that...And, lastly, to my bello and to Rocket—one present and one past... and I am grateful for every moment... daily.

Table of Contents

The Early Years

Year 1 Living Abroad

Year 2 Living Abroad

A Moment in Time

Book II: Year 3 Living Abroad (Excerpts)

The Early Years
1. Naples Taxi Ride

"*Sinistra o destra...? Sinistra* or *destra....?*" What? We had no idea what was just asked of us – or where we were. Specifically, we were in Naples – that, Amber and I, were 100% confident of ... while both a decade apart in experiences lived and bound by close family ties for as long, we were both novice to the scene: Europe. She – a blossoming year of 20 – and me, an inquisitive *anno*[1] of 30... I guess that we were one and the same, in that respect... "*LEFT OR RIGHT?!!*" we surmised that the driver was screaming at us – *sinistra o destra*? and we pointed that way ... we were correct. "Thank God," I thought aloud. And I knew not how many times I would saying be that during those first days, hours... even moments...in Italia.

The first moment of realization of what had just happened to me was utter panic and disbelief from our hosts. "Spaccanapoli[2]?" *utters Tanya – our hostess, sister of Amber, and sidekick of mine of years past. So she can ask me questions with a tonality reserved for undisciplined children.* "You left your bag in the taxi that just went away... do you know where this is?? Do you know where we are?" *Where we were was in the heart of the* Quartiere Spagnolo *– the old Spanish Quarter – of Naples where the passageways are of cobblestone and not designed for vehicle use, where generations of families can be seen either through a window looking upon you or on the same mode of transportation here: the* Vespa[3]. *Not that there aren't many little or tattered cars in this quarter – they are all just small and tattered, and for good reason.* This is the

---

[1] *Anno.* Year (of age).
[2] *Spaccanapoli*, an avenue that slices through the center of Naples, carving the Spanish Quarter from the historic center, and the historic center from more recent development. *Spaccare* – Italian for "to cleave."
[3] *Vespa* – as I learn later – is Italian for *wasp*. The swarms of them buzzing through the quartieri balancing families atop will always be seared into memories from that first arrival.

neighborhood where the secret police do remind silly people like our initial selves to remove their fancy wristwatches and put them in their pockets. And then they smile and speed away on the motorbikes[4]…

"What color was the taxi that dropped you off?" screamed Alexandre.

"Why?" I ask.

"There *is* a *big* difference." He had Generoso on the line and neither was in the mood for questions from me. They wanted answers … actions.

A call was made and a miracle was performed – and again I'm feeling that there's definitely a God to be thanking, as everything was returned to me in perfect order. Miracles *do* happen in Naples… this wasn't the first time, I'm sure. And it wasn't going to be the last time for me – in actuality, it was the beginning of what I had not even begun to imagine as my odyssey that continues to this day. *Sometimes, when we return to a place, a region so familiar that we know our past association was real – very real. When everything is new but utterly so comfortable and familiar, when every new turn isn't really so new – that was Naples for me from the moment I got out of the White taxi cab… I knew that I had returned home.*

Our first days living in the heart of Spaccanapoli was definitely a fast-track to southern Italian life and culture – Naples culture – of which there are few finer. The Spanish had a great influence here. The Greeks. The Moors. *Even the Vikings may have had their time in the sun here … la dolce vita for everyone it seemed over the millennia. It was – and remains – a melting pot of peoples and colors and sounds for me. Seeing wild-caught fish from the local waters and fresh meats from the hills above being sold in stalls next to fine Italian linens and faux*

---

[4] Note *motorbike* not branded *Vespa*, motorcycle, car, or any other vehicle transport labeled with *Polizia*, *Carabinieri*, or any other official markings. These are street vehicles that look as if they had been lifted from a careless previous owner forgetting their keys in the ignition switch.

couture purses – and blending together just fine. That's Naples... sometimes a contradiction in terms but always one of the queens of the old cities of Europe.

The Early Years

2. En Route to the Coast

My next encounter with Generoso, beyond that whirlwind visit at the Caffe Gambrinus[5], was our drive to the Amalfi Coast... I arrived first with Generoso and the gang somehow found their way later... Alex had a garden project to attend to, if I recall... and I'm pretty sure that I am right... You see, Alex always had a garden to attend, and I learned much about passion for plants, animals, and elegance from Alexandre during those first years of my third 12-year cycle around the sun... those special years when there's so much world out there to learn about... Alex was my guide those early years...and he really taught this California kid a great deal about what lay beyond its borders. Alexandre Von Pichler from the south of France... testing the waters of Santa Barbara... we were young, I was in love and, for now, I'll leave it at that...

I may as well start from the beginning... not the real beginning—who really knows where that starting point is... this life... that life... some life in between?? I will say with certainty that this space was familiar from the beginning—the very beginning... from the point where one first begins to round the bend above the Bay of Naples and top the hill as it slopes down and begins to round the bend at the spine of the Sorrentine Peninsula at Colli San Pietro and your lungs are the first to tell your body that something has changed for the better—before your eyes have a chance to even confirm the news... the visual is spellbinding, to say the least—but, most accurate in its assessment....

---

[5] *Caffe Gambrinus* is a Naples establishment – the see-and-be-seen scene. Situated at the edge of the Piazza Plebiscito and across from the Palazzo Reale, it is the iconic, Old World, multifaceted gathering place for the elite and tourists alike – a proper tearoom, a coffeehouse, a bar, a gelateria, a pasticcerria... all supported by a completely competent kitchen and army of seriously uniformed waiters.

Little did I know that first village that I saw rounding the bend—perched in the distance there so perfectly—would become our home for the next 20 years... much like in Naples then (and much like now), this place still draws me to tears at a moment's notice and I still feel like I am coming or leaving home every time that moment presents itself. I never have written to you during the autumn, and I've been having a hard time finding my muse to regale you in such a grand tale... such a story... and such a true one at that. But I am suddenly feeling that this is now indeed the time to regale you of those first years—those inspirational and guiding years that led me to where I am now and exactly how we found and fell in love with this magical and storied coast and this utterly perfect village and this particular hillside of the most special part of our village... perhaps she's always been my muse and I just didn't quite understand it fully then and as some of you know fully well already (and some of you will come to), she's had my absolute attention (the land of our village hillside) for many a year now. Different old villas and different gardens. But we started with one of the most grand of *grandes dames* along the entire coast and I had no idea how my expectations were about to be so exceeded. Perhaps it was my lack of expectation that saved me—*non lo so.*

With Generoso at the wheel, one could only focus on the road and knowing which way to brace for the turns... but we arrived at our destination down the coast... past Positano and her stunning architectural achievement and testament to Italian geometry and physics... past the famed Hotel San Pietro and eventually to a little section of the coast—to that little spot with the best view imaginable and the tower[6] on the water and at our new casa. I also had no idea that our little casa was, in actuality, a great villa. But everything of value and substance happens in small, metered out doses here on the coast... that's nature and that's reality in the people's nature here... *piano,*

---

[6] Saracen Towers – construction begun by the Normans in the 11th century and continued by their Spanish viceroys centuries later – more than 300 dot the coast of the Campania Region, originally constructed as watchtowers to monitor movements of potentially invading Saracens (used at the time to refer to Arab Muslims).

6

piano (slowly, slowly)—it's how you take the walking paths and stairs and how you take life and meeting new folk... *piano, piano*... I wish I could have known that term earlier when driving that road with Generoso—Generoso during that period of his life did absolutely zero activities slowly—driving to say the least. But we arrived somewhere on a hill with the most stellar vista of Capri and Positano and a blazing hot sun! It is late October now and that blazing sun, she still has my back.... *Andiamo*... let's go...

The Early Years

3. Our Second June at the Villa

It was June 2001. At the villa... la casa di Generoso.

Wednesday, June 6th

Our house has all of the great idiosyncrasies one would expect from a grand old villa. For starters, one has to hold the toilet handle, just so, in order for things to stay in order. And if you open the wrought-iron front door the wrong way (as Bello did), you pay to have the metal worker (operaio) to come and assess, contemplate a method for repair, and determine a possible date for a return visit—in our case, a one-week feat. But that was last year... the door is working just fine now, so far, so good. I'll go out to the terrace and assess the state of things—the terrace is a great barometer for what's transpired around the villa during the past season or two... Things look good... something must be up... because they didn't look like this last year...

Thursday, June, 7th

Day two at the villa and already my hands are beginning to hurt. I think I will have to graduate beyond a pair of old schoolhouse scissors if I'm going to have my way with this ancient wisteria and its counterpart bougainvillea—they both are screaming for some constructive sculpting and I'd really like to frame the vista of Capri and Positano. But these two plants have other plans—they will thank me when I'm done. It's raining, again, and the sun is shining... now that's a proper June shower, wouldn't you say...? The church bells ring every 15 minutes around here... at least *our* church bells do. I don't know if I can think of anything more beautiful to comment on at the moment.

Friday, June 8th

Day three at the villa... it rained last night—a really hard thunderstorm that seemed to originate from our terrace. It is no wonder everything is either stone, metal, or bolted down around here... and this morning, it's as if nothing ever happened, unless you are garden obsessed, that is...

Our villa has many players—it's a grand old place and there are several "apartments" that are anything but—think little mini-villas, with soaring ceilings that drip peeling fresco chips on you on occasion and with makeshift kitchens and bathrooms. And they are all very interesting these neighbors of ours and seem to come from a layer of society that isn't quite aristocratic but seems a little lofty in origin—the bells are ringing again... I really like this place...

And somehow six years pass. And somehow Bello and I managed to have our third week of June at the villa... until that last day in May in 2005 when we were not leaving for the entire month.

And in those early years—when all year we only dreamed of coming for our one glorious week at that magical space—we forged, ever so slowly, a close-knit bond with our seasonal families of the Villa Marchese. From all parts of Italy they came: When the wind changed from the north and came from the south, that brought downstairs lady Ballarati from Tuscana... and, later, her brood—who we love so much... Catarina's mother was a guest of the family many years earlier of the lady of the current lady of the house. We are all guests here at the villa. Guests who do pay their own way—but guests in every sense of the word nevertheless. (Some lessons we had yet to learn...) And also with the change of weather, upstairs would arrive Giuliana and Stefano from Apulia... Giuliana with her tales of better homemaking for me I had yet to know, and Stefano and his early years' inquisitive glance that warmed up to being so much more as time went on. Our host, Generoso, was at that time our patron saint. He always will deserve that status. He made sure of that from the onset. He delivers babies for a living in Naples and has one very respectable family vineyard of his surname: di Meo. We were invited for repeat performances at the theatre Villa Marchese by his good graces and I was determined to make certain during those early years that we would continue to be. Sharing our grand terrace (one of the best of the village) was one man of Naples who we never saw... but his children, later, often. It seemed that membership to the

Villa Club had some preconceived expectations: family included. We were already that big exception—and that did not go without notice in my eyes. So, from day one, we made ourselves useful. Very. Membership does have its price beyond the obvious when you are the Americans being allowed and accepted into such a space, I figured. And we spent many years cleaning and clearing gardens to that point. I guess that's still my motivation. I now have that same affliction towards our entire village.... But a villa doesn't stop at its 3-foot thick interior walls, no, no ... they never do. We had neighbors and grounds and past battles that our host family had seeded that we had no idea of at that moment in time. You see, old wounds are like grand old villas —bandages really don't get to the root of a problem—they just cover it up. Yet another layer of plaster and paint with hopes for the best. But, eventually, the situation represents itself again. Another lesson later learned...

Ladies of Toscana

We had a lovely first night catching up with Benedetta (Bendi) and her now husband, Federico (Feddy)—*sans* daughter this weekend. Catarina and her mum in Toscana are holding down their ship and I'm sure that they are having an excellent time. We love Bendi and Feddy—he is an architect by trade and his aunt wrote that fabulous, epic culinary bible: *La Cucina Napolitana*. A must read—even if it isn't available in English. EPIC. Bendi is much like her mother and the countless generations of women that hail from their region. Taste exudes but in the most simple of expressions. Being brash isn't the Toscana lady way.... being flawless is. Bendi made us a great pasta of fresh tomatoes and fusilli—that was it—but so delicious. *Al dente* pasta, of course. Women from that region don't require much to make something become so much... and Bendi and Feddy stayed another night... that was nice. We didn't see them before they parted. But I do know this—two months later there was an announcement of a new addition to the pack... I just smiled and felt a small part of a bigger picture for once here. Our host family is beyond steeped with complexities—they are a foundation to solidarity of a different sort I would later come to learn. Solidarity from the inside looking out. At that point, I was only looking in... I had (and still have) so much to learn... don't we all... But, I digress...

Year 1 Living Abroad

4. Spring has sprung... and my houseguest has departed...

... It was my fabulously sweet girlfriend, Hannah, who left yesterday morning at 4:30.... The skies were already dramatic and the lights shining from Positano off the sea seemed almost unreal and she cried. I know exactly how she felt. For years I cried upon leaving the coast. Now I live here and every moment has the potential to make me feel like weeping. This morning was no exception—for mythical moments abound here when it comes to the weather and apparently this time of year it is the fiercest. For those of you that skipped Philosophy 101 (or just read the CliffsNotes as I did), this is the fabled land of Homer's three sirens from *The Odyssey*—the very spot from which these famous maidens would draw passing ships in close with the intoxicating singing and crash them on the rocks and drown all the sailors... I wish I could regale you further, but alas, I only read the CliffsNotes—but believe me when I tell you that the sound is like nothing you have ever heard—both frightening and exciting and kind of seductive. We do have the real thing here, *The Odyssey*, though and I plan to pick it up soon, I'm pretty busy keeping up with the dogs, my Bello, the villa and the grounds at this particular point in time.

Hannah and I spent the Easter weekend rearranging the villa's great room and our sitting room. The great room measures about 15'x 35' and was such an opposing space that everyone was compelled to sit in the sitting room—seems logical—but that, in fact, would drive me crazy (of course) because the sitting room (although the view over Capri is stellar) opens onto the bedroom and that is where Jackie spends about 20 hours a day/night sleeping in front of her heater. (She and Rocket are cuddled side-by-side as I write.) Although her days are definitely waning (and it breaks my heart), I take comfort in the words of Buddha and realize that this is simply a shell she is in at present and her soul will continue and comeback to us again. Dogs (and animals, in general) seem to have a more of a grasp of this than we people do. I think that is why we humans get so worked up when a loved one departs. The loved one is off on a new adventure and is probably not that upset about leaving a failing body—but it still breaks my heart. To tell you the truth, Jackie is the real reason that we came—if I had to really boil it down. Although the perils abound around here for an aging dog with cataracts, less then perfect hearing (she can hear you but just often can't discern from exactly where your voice is coming from) and a pulled leg that occasionally gets re-pulled causing her excruciating pain, she has Rocket to retrieve her in the garden and right her way (she REALLY appreciates him) and she has my attention 24/7. Now, back to Hannah...

Hannah is my neighbor in Santa Barbara, sidekick, and all-around good friend. She had the courage to actually come to the South of Italy and spend four days alone with me and my many neuroses. This shouldn't surprise most of you: my neurosis. But Hannah is a patient sort. She would make an appropriate suggestion regarding moving some item in the villa and I would (of course) immediately retort with "Oh. No. We can't do that... blah, blah, blah....” and usually within ten minutes whatever was suggested was being done—this dance went on for days. What we did, eventually, accomplish was removing most of the seating in the sitting room (same size as great room and both with ceilings higher than a two-story building and as difficult to heat), and added them to the two existing chairs next to the fireplace in the great room. Hannah then pulled out fabulous thing after fabulous thing from who knows where and we did some thoughtful editing and before long the great room was looking pretty GREAT and my sitting room was much more of a sitting room for two—in a huge space. Now it feels like an old, big villa. Picture hearing someone coming from the back wing by their clicking shoes a full 30 seconds before they enter the room and you get the mood... by Day 3 (it was a rainy weekend) we had gone through many bottles of Prosecco and loads of espresso—typically not in that order—and Hannah had graduated on to the kitchen, back wing foyer, and her bathroom... had she had another week I am sure we would have started rearranging the other parts of the villa, too...

Change

Here, everyone knows where everyone else's keys are hidden and it is a very tight-knit group. We are the upstarts with only 12 years (10 with my bello) here, although we have earned our position with sweat and tears and a good old-fashioned dose of respect for the owners and their place. And a little change is a constant, even in the life of an old villa. Seeing the spring come moment-by-moment drives that home. Watching my old dog change daily drives home that exact same point. I recently told a young friend of mine heading off to college that we are each living our movie and she should remember that there are no retakes. Nature and the cycle of life seem know this.

Today, I am either going to call and have Salvatore come and fix the bloody washing machine's spin cycle or I will do a round of hand washing yet again.... My girlfriend Sally's suggestion of soaking the clothes in the tub overnight with washing soap and baking soda seems pretty good... I'm curious to see how it works. Knowing Sally—who does not regularly hand wash her family's clothes in the bathtub but is the savviest hostess I know—it will work splendidly. There is a laundry only 200 yards down the hill but that is too easy, and why be predictable, right?

Jackie is up for her 8:00 a.m. snack... this time an advanced formula treat of Glucosamine, MSM (?) & Chondroitin for her hips and joints... Rocket heard her eating something and has chimed in too. Time to recharge the computer...

Falling Walls, the Weather, and Real Working Class Italians

Ciao bello/bella,

I thought it befitting of a time to write you—the weather has turned from worse (actually, that depends on how you interpret it, I guess) to even worse and we are in for an early cocktail hour. I purchased a whole chicken this morning (impulse purchase while passing the *macelleria*[7]) and it has been stuffed with onions from the neighbor's garden up above (the same neighbors with the donkeys coming later this week right through what is to be my new vegetable garden, but more of that in a moment) and I've been given a nice bottle of red wine by Luca, who is son #3 of the family above.

This—the gift of wine—occurred while Rocket and I were waiting out an unexpected downpour that happened while we were passing their place on the way home from our hike. Their whole house is under total remodel – with boulders and dirt and earth and old tile and just construction stuff all over the place and for three levels, it was really nice of him to offer both the tour—and the libation. I will depart from the norm of Prosecco this evening and have their *vino* with the *gallo*[8] (soon to be *pollo*, cooked chicken) tonight. Prosecco for now though... And *domani*[9], I will bring the neighbors a lovely box of citrus—the oranges are superb right now—I know this because I was feeling a little low of energy this afternoon and I had noticed one of the orange trees in the formal garden (that's what I call it because it is the most manicured portion of the main walk) was a heavily laden fruit tree with oranges in one section, so I climbed it and picked a bag full of fruit and promptly squeezed a couple of pints and of juice and drank it *subito* (right away). It was about as perfect as a thing can be. I just realized something funny: I only know their first names—the family above—and I've only had conversations with them separately over the years. Long conversations, actually—and tours. They say they're related... and they do look alike... Mamma Maria (she works the terraces all day), Pop-pop (he runs the fish store with his buddies); Domenico (son #1, and all that comes with that, inclusive of the pretty wife); Giulio (son #2 who does the purchasing for the family fish business pre-dawn in Sorrento daily

---

[7]*Macellaria*. Butcher shop. A must-visit for any authentic costierra visit. Be prepared for some serious animal husbandry in full display – and some really good cuts of meat.
[8] *Gallo*. Rooster
[9] *Domani*. Tomorrow. A *domani* generally translates to "until tomorrow" which in actuality can refer to any time or date in the future, but not today.

AND is flawlessly remodeling and old olive press adjacent to our place in the most authentic and artistic of manners, conserving the old press and making it part of his new six-room Bed & Breakfast), and Luca (son #3 who works the land with Maria in the afternoons and in the early mornings takes fish up to Agerola[10] to sell).[11]

Luca and our Alberto (our *giardiniere*[12] of sorts) are buddies, apparently, and Alberto tells me that Luca loves to come up to his place, in Agerola, on occasion for a cold beer (the third son isn't the ultimate place to be positioned around here—you have to work really hard but Luca makes the best of it.)

The Arrival of the Ass Man and his Hard-working Mules

The Gagliano's garden is about the same size as this garden (four terraces approximately 125-150 yards long), minus the villa. It is all grapes, vegetables, weeds, peas, artichokes, more weeds, flowers, figs, oranges, and assorted blossoming trees. These are real working class/middle class Italians. They put in a long day. Oh, and last month, their new fancy wall at the B&B project completely caved in on the garden directly below next to ours, so they are going to be bringing a bunch of mules through my new vegetable garden next week to begin the repairs. Lovely. They first have to remove the tons and tons of rocks and rubble and then begin the rebuilding process (which is slated to take two months) because the crew only works after their regular job. (Who knew asses were in such high demand...? But they are.) And to access this property, from the road above, the ass-man and his crew constructed ramps with scaffolding, poles, and timber to breach terrace upon terrace (this is for mules with heavy loads) until ultimately reaching our place and then, from there, they will have to cross my

---

[10] *Agerola* is a mountain village high above the coast famous for its *fior di latte*, a fresh mozzarella made from cow's milk symbolic of the coast. Although close as the crow flies, it takes nearly 45 minutes for a car to scale the switchbacks of the only road to the top.

[11] Spoiler alert: there are actually four Gagliano sons, I just was not aware at that point of the number or the order.

[12] *Giardiniere.* Gardener

vegetable garden to the neighboring garden. It is even longer and more difficult then it sounds. Crazy. But, what is one to do except accommodate? Especially when I've been asked to do so. Thank God nobody was under the wall when it went. Walls are a big deal these days in Montebello. It seems that someone's wall fell on someone else's head last year somewhere here in Italy and the wall's owner was held liable and was sent to prison. Now, everyone is paranoid about their aging walls and the town is backlogged with repair requests—hence the busy mules. And to make matters even more complicated, if one lives on a *via* (footpath) with recently remodeled stairs (as we do), then no mules are allowed on those stairs—meaning you have to negotiate with your neighbors to ingress/egress their garden with your pack of mules. An apparently totally normal consideration. (This is why I love it here so much.)

Stasera (This Evening)[13]

Our evening chicken has been on for 30 minutes and is beginning to brown ... I'll add carrots in 30 minutes... time to build a fire... laundry is on the line.... I guess it will be all the fresher when it dries tomorrow for it is raining, yet again...

Starting fires now isn't such a daunting of a task as it was when Hannah and I were figuring it out and the learning curve was much steeper. I do feel somewhat inadequate for using the fire starters though—but I am getting over it. (The lingering smell of creosote on one's fingers even after washing is somewhat disconcerting though, but this is Italy.)

Candles are the next layer of mood... and Angela finally received cream-colored candles, as opposed to the white. I find a cream-colored candle illuminates such a nicer color then do the white.... Angela and her husband, Salvatore, run the alimentari[14] *where I do most our shopping.*

---

[13] *Stasera*. This evening. Regardless of the time of year, evening represents the hours post the three o'clock hour.

[14] *Alimentari*. The closest translation would be grocery, but *Alimentari Angela* serves as an all-purpose store – fresh produce, cheese, meats, dry goods, household necessities, social gathering point, latest local news distribution

My bello, on the other hand, shops the entire village :-) I shop Angela's because they deliver. And when I do venture out it is always with the dogs and we live hundreds of steps up from Angela's. Jackie needs to be carried up stairs: you do the math. Their son, Luca (there are ten names for guys here and Luca is one of them), has a beautiful wife (named Rossina), a young son (Salvatore), and brand-new baby daughter (Angela – here one names their first son after the grandfather and the first daughter after the grandmother) and runs his own gym during the "off season" for locals AND delivers for his family's store. Although last night, Salvatore met me at the bottom of our stairs with the forgotten bag of dairy from the day's earlier delivery—he was riding on his absolutely fabulous vintage Vespa, in his even more fabulous old cashmere, baby-blue sweater—total class. Here, taste abounds, even on the most pedestrian of levels. Our groceries were delivered—to the kitchen—while I was in the garden in a tree pruning an old arbor that I, unwittingly, severed the old-growth jasmine vine from last fall when I was a bit over zealous with my new pruners. (Think 20 years of over-growth.) It will look stellar in the coming year(s). Sometimes you have to make some hard choices around here between immediate aesthetic satisfaction and long-term betterment of the villa, and, sometimes, you just make a bad cut. This was the latter.

... The fire is roaring, the carrots are in the oven and I am chiming out. It's 7 p.m. More with my 7 a.m. espresso... but, Luca's red wine is really tasty, f.y.i. Glad that your here with me, right now. At least in my thoughts. JJ

La Giornata[15] (The Day)

.... Up at 6:45 for the pooches and they are now both cuddled together in Jackie's bed—predictable. Here, a foregone conclusion isn't such a bad thing when it is something that you're enjoying. At home I loathe

---

point – all within a 15 x 30 foot space with Angela at the helm. The sliding vertical door opens directly onto the only road through the coast and it is often blocked in the summer with buses from opposite directions trying to navigate a road with the width of a country lane.

[15] *La Giornata*. The day, representing the daytime elements.

the thought, but here it means that everything is *tutto posto*[16] (as it should be). Jackie seems to be doing much better with the stairs and negotiating the right ways to travel the grounds. I don't have to follow her about as in the early weeks here. Yesterday, she and Rocket had haircuts. Rocket had a full Mohawk going on and it was getting gross. Jackie tolerated a bit of a cut because she knew treats were in store... she then had a lovely hot bath and she actually danced around the entire villa afterwards. She was dancing, spinning around, running about—apparently she really needed a bathing... the family up above have a dog named Gregorio (Greg for locals) who is an Irish something or other and isn't the brightest bulb in the shop but has a heart of gold. His family lets him run about the garden, but when Gregorio comes to visit us there are rules. Of course there are. There is no "unnecessary" barking—leaving room for their own interpretation—because dogs do speak to one another here with much more acceptance and impunity then in the States. Sometimes Jackie goes to the upper *orto*[17] and simply barks to other dogs... they all do it. Rocket isn't a barker though—unless it is regarding a cat or a stranger on the grounds, then he goes ballistic.

And my Bello.... you may ask.... he's on a plane right now returning from the States. He had an appointment at an Air Force base in the Midwest—I am not allowed to say—this week. He was gone for four days. That would be like coming to Italy for *pranzo*[18] and then returning to California the next day. He is going to be home for the next ten days! After a week or so, he likes to bust out of here... this place is remote, if you haven't gotten the gist.

Today I am going to deal with the laundry above (I am hoping that it will be a hot day) and wash the bedding and hang that to dry.... first I need to install another clothesline—the existing is already full. After that, I

---

[16] *Tutto posto.* Literally "everything placed" used to signify "all right."
[17] *Orto.* Vegetable garden – as opposed to a floral or flower garden. Clearly gardens with different intentions and rarely do the two mix.
[18] *Pranzo.* Lunch. *Pranzo* is basically how a fancy lunch with several courses – and with guests arriving perhaps – is referred.

will most likely do some quick gardening (I like all the paths perfect at least every other day), pick some oranges for friends (already pressed and consumed a pint before espresso), and shave before Bello comes home. I look like Grizzly Adams—sort of. I do have the carcass from last night's chicken (minus the breasts—Bello only eats white meat) that I will turn into a lovely chicken stock (can't buy it in stores) and put in the freezer for future risotto. I'll start that slow-cooking process in a moment—after my second coffee (it takes both working burners on the stove to warm the milk and espresso). (My kitchen needs its own, dedicated note for one to really get the picture...)

Il Giardino [19] (The Garden)

And the garden: well, the wisteria is as if it's on steroids and the roses are beginning to pop. I've liberated all of the citrus trees on the lower two terraces and the grumpy old uncle hasn't caught me in the act personally, but I have been spotted by neighbors—most of whom are delighted to see this feral part of the garden (that is fully visible from the village) cleaned up after so many years. There is this awful and thorny bush that spreads like wildfire and covers everything—even fruit trees—and eventually kills the tree unless removed. And to remove this plant you have to first cut away at the entire bush, remove that, let it dry for a few days, and then go for the root system. If you don't remove the roots then the plant is back in two weeks—rain or not. It is simply awful. Oh, and if you scratch yourself on the plant be prepared to wake up in the middle of the night itching like a mad man for two or three nights... I wear heavy, armor-like, attire for this task. And I try to blend in with the foliage because Grumpy has been merely yards away on his terrace when I've been cleaning and pruning.... it is like a really odd comedy. I did discover that the sour orange tree (actually the tree was decapitated ten years ago during the feud and now it is comprised of five perfect shoots) is in actuality a fabulous tangerine tree. The fruit is enormous and getting very sweet. Fortunately, I have the only keys to the gate that access this part of the villa... I also discovered a peach tree

---

[19] *Il Giardino*. The Garden. Not to be confused with any garden containing vegetables; fruit trees, however, can contribute to *il giardino*.

that is a remnant of the older peach trees from the terrace above. This tree is about 6 years old and has a bunch of flowers, so there should be good peaches in a couple of months... the fig trees have had their bases freed from weeds and morning glory—which is the other great nemesis of the garden and moi.

... It is just now 8 a.m. I hear Jackie's claws clicking about the villa, no doubt looking for me, and another treat. Rocket is back in bed—our bed. To be a teenager living in Italy...

Baci ed abbracci[20],

James

The Arrival of the Asses, the Fireflies, and Our New Washing Machine

An update from last week—I wasn't able to get this to you...

I know it is a bit soon for another of my seemingly endless dissertations, but there is always something of interest happening around here that I feel compelled to share it with you... But first, Bello just arose—the dogs are driving him nuts—so I best get his coffee on.... we are either going to Amalfi (to Pasticcceria Pansa, one of the best pastry shops on the Coast) or to Sorrento (best and only spa in the area) today.... and on a side note: my clothes washer is finally repaired! What a delight it is to put articles of clothing in a machine and have them come out clean and spun... how quickly we forget (and subsequently appreciate) the importance of the accouterment of life.... second coffee in hand...

Well, the other night the fireflies arrived. Much like the evening bats, they arrived in mass—safety in numbers, perhaps, or just better chances in getting lucky. I can see how the bats figure it out—they all live together in a cave—but the fireflies all reside in different flowers and separate sections of the garden and they somehow know exactly when to emerge onto the scene. The visits are fleeting both in the particular time of the evening (dusk) that they appear and the early part

---

[20] *Baci ed abbracci.* Kisses and hugs

of the spring that they make their presence known. (Our first year—together here at the villa—Bello and I witnessed their arrival and we hadn't seen but a fly or two since then due to our normal visit in June, when their season is waning—so this has been special.) When you sit on the terrace at night you can see the flies dancing about in the dark, some 40 yards away in the distance—it is something to witness. I guess they (fireflies) are common on the East Coast—but being a California guy they were/are something new altogether.

Some further updates:

The asses are getting closer to arriving. I see that the ramp they will scale (I do mean scale because the slope seems to be at 20 degrees) has been completed and is in the middle of my *orto*. Alberto and I are building a complete corridor for them to follow as to not completely destroy all that we've done so far in preparation for the tomatoes and eggplant plants that are sitting on the porch now. My hands are a disaster.

Baci bella,

JJ

...e che differenza fa una settimana! (...and what a difference a week makes!)

At home (in the States), a week represents one quarter of the time in between mortgage and car payments, the amount of time one waits between the week's end and the number of days (7) that we Americans think about work. Here, the same issues are still relevant but the similarities stop right about there. Bello is back in the states—third trip in six weeks—the U.S. Customs folks are beginning to wonder about him and his secret agent mystique is growing. (I, too, sometimes wonder if all this environmental/conservation, saving-the-planet-talk is really true or simply his front... I've never met a work colleague, even once, and the "office" in Santa Barbara is conveniently void of other "personnel" whenever I've visited...) Well, as long as those weekly details of reality are competently dealt with, then I guess I have nothing to gripe about.

He has assured me (after a hellacious 24 hours with me not so pleased about this trip) that the travels will contract to a low roar—as in less then a week away at a time... I'm logging the days, so we'll see. In either case though, I am trying not to become a complete monster about it and remember exactly where it is that I find myself at present. Where WE are at present.

Nipote di Tanya: Nicolas (Tanya's Nephew)

So on to this past week... Bello left for Santa Barbara last Saturday (mortgage time) and is now in San Juan continuing the organization of a multi-billion-dollar (five-year) project, which is why he travels there on a monthly basis. In the interim, I've been amused with hosting my girlfriend Tanya's nephew, Nick (Nico)—he's 23. You must remember Tanya – from our first moments in Naples after *that* taxi ride... Tanya and I go way back and her family was very instrumental in my development as a person during those influential 20-something years. I used to live in Tanya's mother's (Ilene's) pool house—this was right before meeting my Bello. Well, in 1997 Amber (Tanya's younger sister) and I came to Europe (my first excursion out of the North America) to visit Tanya and Alexandre who were living in Naples at the time. They resided in the heart of old Naples (*Spaccanapoli*), and when I say "old," I really cannot emphasize that enough. Streets are swept at dawn with palm fronds, one is forbidden to remove their trash during daylight hours, and there had better be someone authorizing your existence there or the local *Camorra* (the original Mafia and very much an integral part of Napolitano society) will simply rob your house. And possibly hurt you. We were safe. Upon arrival I mistakenly left my carry-on bag in the taxi (complete with passport and cash, favorite glasses – accessories were very important to me then-- and MY PASSPORT!!!) Well, Alexandre and Tanya immediately called their friend and protector, Generoso, who immediately called the "white taxi" company (there are two companies that rival for fares in Naples and are designated by the color of their vehicle) and within five minutes my bag was delivered back to *Spaccanapoli*. It was nothing short of miraculous. Now, Tanya lives in Florence with Paolo and they have baby Sofia to take care of... plus there work worlds and life... Alexandre I hear is traveling about (again)

24

and Generoso is still my protector – in a funny way, I guess. He is the unofficial third child of the Marchese's... more like godchild I would say. I'm guessing that Gene delivered Vivianna and Luigi (who goes by "Lui")—he's delivered half of Naples. (I'm also guessing that is why my valuables were returned so straightaway.) So you see—if it weren't for Tanya I wouldn't have met Generoso, wouldn't have come to the villa and wouldn't have met some of the most important people of my life— including Bello (had I not met Generoso and we had not gone to Capri, then I wouldn't have met Antonio (18 months of crazy back-and-forth and a crazy Italian relationship), thus leaving me ready for the relationship of my life now, and even inadvertently in meeting some of you. (We are the sum of our experiences... and some of you booked me for your events because of my experiences... funny how life puts people and places together and we are to make what we make of it...) So, that is how Nico came about being my guest—what comes around most often goes around, eventually. I think he had a good time. Claudia (my savior on a regular basis and my local Camorra protector) and I took Nico on an Amalfi-to-Positano chocolate and gelato tour, we hiked the Path of the Gods trail and Nico helped me plant the entire vegetable *orto*. We sat up late, drank prosecco, and regaled each other in our realities about being 23 and 42. You should try hanging out with someone half your age for a couple of days sometime—you can learn a lot about your own perspectives. Now he's off to Paris. And I am alone at the villa until Saturday—when Bello returns.

The asses have yet to arrive for the wall repair, but it is consistently the same story: *presto, forse questo fine settimana*[21]. Much like a broken record. Speaking of records...Nico and I set up the turntable and speakers and played some great classics... Stan Getz, Gilberto, Space Odyssey 2001... out there... then we re-worked and cleaned out the bar in the great room—polished the crystal decanters and tried to figure out the various *digestivos* and *aperativi* by smell, color and eventually some tasting—but it was morning so tastes were limited to finger dips... I had no idea that one could make digestivos from things like artichokes. We

---

[21] *Presto, forse questo fine settimana*. Soon, perhaps this weekend

didn't taste that one though—it smelled suspicious.

Il Giardino, le Galline, and a Grumpy Zio (The Garden, the Chickens, and the Grumpy Uncle)

The orto now consists of 45 giant strawberries (apparently, one has to either place hair nets on each plant or fence them all in due to the local lizard's acquired taste for sweets); 40 (or so) eggplants; 10 zucchini plants; 40 *basilico*[22]; loads (40-50) of *pomodori e pomodorini*[23]; and a mixture of parsley and celery (they look identical at ½ an inch and I inadvertently mixed them up...); plus the arugula that grows wild and the artichokes that I planted two weeks ago. Now I guess I wait for everything to grow. Alberto is bringing me five (female) chickens tomorrow or the next day (both debatable, in actuality). With the chicken coop finally being cleaned out, it seemed a waste not to have fresh eggs and fluffy birds about. It should be interesting training Rocket not to want to kill them and to see Jackie try to catch them... I am told, they (the chickens) need to be secured at night for fear of wild dogs (of a sort) from coming down from the hills to try to eat them—according to Alberto. I've two days to complete the repairs. I now know why all the old beds (100% metal) were tossed on top of the original chicken coop—to keep the vermin out... oh well. So today, I will work on the coop, bury my water line to the *orto* (as to not have to view the line above ground) and work on the secret garden path. Speaking of which... *the grumpy uncle and aunt below* have resorted to their binoculars in their attempt to see exactly what is going on up here (they sit and stare for minutes and minutes at a time and I, sincerely, wave back). I can see their reasoning a bit—this was her grandmother's and mother's house and here I am in it... but they treat the Marchese's with complete disrespect, so I am not overtly friendly, just respectful of where she may be coming from. Her husband has no blood claim to the land and shouldn't be such an ass about it all though... in my humble opinion. But I'm not here to judge. I've successfully (as in I haven't been caught) cleared the path below through the secret garden so that I may access

---

[22] *Basilico.* Basil
[23] *Pomodori e pomodorini.* Tomatoes and cherry tomatoes

the roses and citrus below and the trees are not being covered in the awful "ick" of a stinging needles bush as they usually are by this time of year, this is what I think perplexes the relatives below—but they just can't quite put their fingers on exactly what is different above... it is all about selective weed pulling and never being seen. If he were to see me it isn't as if he can really do a thing about it. I figure why fuel the fire though and it is fun to watch them so perplexed... no harm is done and at least the trees below can breathe this year. And if you don't keep up on the "ick" and the morning glory (what a stupid name), then the upper terraces become inundated and that then requires all one's attention in the summer to maintain. (I plan on going to the shore more often this spring with my Bello.)

✳✳✳✳✳✳✳✳✳✳✳✳✳✳✳✳✳✳✳

What else... it is midnight for you... time for a possible second "round" of espresso for me and to check to clothes on the line—from yesterday. I hope that we didn't have one of those awful *scirocco* rains[24] from Africa last night—they bring in the Sahara dust and EVERYTHING is covered in fine, sand-like soot. Enough to drive one completely nuts unless you're willing to just get over it. You never really know what happens during the evening hours until you actually go out and investigate the grounds.

Perhaps this evening I will have Claudia, Barbara (she and her fiancé, Antonio, run boat tours), and Raimondo (Barbara's older brother and major renaissance man like Alberto) over for a bite... or later in the week. These things take time to arrange because no one actually answers their phone— they eventually return your call by text and there is no voicemail. I'm just as guilty—if not egregious—just ask my Bello.

The cell is rarely on and has developed this habit of turning itself off, or simply not ringing. (Bello tried me last night with the phone right next to

---

[24] The *scirocco* starts as a dry, hot, dusty, northerly wind originating over the Sahara but can eventually gather speed and carry more humidity as it blows over the Mediterranean into southern Europe, often bringing heavy rain laden with desert sand.

me—he had to call the house line). And the house phone has a short cord that requires me to sit at the phone desk to speak—seems to make sense, if you think about it. So, subsequently, if you try me on the house line I had best be walking past the phone (I keep the volume on the lowest setting as to not run the risk of waking Jackie from one of her many naps).

And the pets: for many of you, this is the best part...

Jackie's eyesight grows weaker each week—she did one of her shortcuts from the entry last night—even with barricades. But she's a trooper. Her new thing is being a watchdog and following me around the garden (when she can keep up) and planting herself wherever I may be. She inevitably falls a sleep in the sun and wakes in a state of delirium. I know her nap timing, so I usually return to where I left her and retrieve her... Rocket helps out a great deal with keeping an eye on her. She still loves the morning, waking up, and her food bowl, and of course the many treat administrations throughout the day. Rocket has discovered the pleasure in chasing balls. He likes to pop them so they fit more comfortably in his mouth but I have yet to successfully explain to him that they do not roll as well when flattened—he's beginning to get it. He likes to leave his favorite ball (most likely absconded with from Gregorio up above, or Giuseppina's leftovers from last summer. Giuseppina is the heir apparent of this place—she's Vivianna's daughter, all of 6, and a handful—she and I will be wrestling for this place in 40 years and I'm afraid to say that I think he'll win, at that time—for now I'm covered.)

I should run... battery running low on my typewriter here—who said writing is dead...? Computers open our worlds to great communicating. And I cannot tell you how much closer and how much I have enjoyed reading about some of your lives as of late. There are some aspects of the modern age that I wouldn't change for a thing. Did I mention the 300 year-old *colombaia*[25] that the villa is built around? Back in the day, that was how one sent messages. And the only person allowed to have

---

[25] *Colombaia*. Pigeon house. Reserved for the most elite of the times, the pigeon houses represented the most modern course for communications at the time and only the most affluent of any village were allowed such power.

a *colombaia* was a landed person (person with land)—ours is the only *colombaia* in all of the village. I am happy to send this note to you the modern way.

Baci e abbracci,

JJ

…. And how quickly May has arrived

Although it seems like an eternity away when there was snow on the hilltops. Bello is back from his latest big trip and promises that there will be no more ten-day excursions—the weather is far too nice for that and he can't wait to get into the sea. He's run out the door (double espresso in hand) to try and catch the 9:30 bus to Positano for banking—Montebello has no bank, just an ATM that seems to only work on occasion.

I'll try to keep this brief, but so much has happened in the past week since my latest update above… The *orto* (vegetable garden) is fully installed—the zucchinis are flowering-- and I've had my first *fragola* (strawberry) eaten by a lizard. The locals warned me of this and now it is war… Rocket has been given a new job. Speaking of which, my little guy has been hopping about on three paws for almost a week now because he crashed into the stone stairs in the garden because he was running too fast and his paws couldn't keep ahead of the stair's incline. He really thrashed the top part of his right paw (right in front of me—he was running to me) and couldn't put weight on it for some time. He's still working it a bit though…. Two nights ago he woke me at 2 a.m. wanting under the covers and he was holding his little paw up… he's a smart boy. He's still in bed. Jackie is out and about… which surprises me due to the tumble to the neighbor's yard that happened last night when out for her late-night pee. (No more late-night strolls without Rocket at her side was the lesson I learned.) She fell a good 12 feet to the neighbor's garden and we found her by listening for her faint cry…. She's absolutely no worse for the wear with the exception of a little cut under her left eye. Thank God, Buddha, Mario, or whomever!!! And speaking of which, today is the one-year anniversary of the passing of Mario

Marchese—whose home we reside in. The Marchese family are coming to Montebello for a special double mass this Sunday—it is the celebration of San Gennaro (the founding father of Montebello) and a tribute to Mario... I've been invited to attend with the family—requested in a subtle way. Afterwards I've invited the entire villa gang, it being a holiday weekend—May Day—everyone is here... (which, is an entirely different tale of descriptive characters) and the family Marchese to *pranzo* (lunch). We'll be doing American tea sandwiches. Egg salad (from my chickens), chicken salad (NOT from my chickens), and *tonno* (tuna) salad. Bread is the difficult ingredient to find on a Sunday, but Bello is on that. The grounds are tidy, roses are in full force (I'll make a bouquet for the grave but will refrain from going to the site and let the family have some alone time) and I have yet to decide exactly where to serve lunch—which terrace.

Some Marchese history (as told to me from Claudia's father over pranzo *at her house last week): apparently, there used to be ten families that ran the show in Cuore del Mare (Montebello is a* frazione[26] *of Cuore del Mare) and the Marchese's were one of them. So much so, that people would tip their caps as a sign of respect when members of the Marchese walked the village. This would be Mario's father and grandfather, for things rapidly changed in the South after the Second World War and democracy was installed. So mass will be interesting because who comes and where they sit and who they greet and all will speak volumes. It is what is implied and not necessarily said that holds water around these parts. I rather like that about this place.*

Pranzo at Claudia's was too much—as in fabulous. Lydia (Claudia's mamma) made fresh ricotta, eggplant parmigiana[27], vegetables, a lemon tort (with lemons from our garden), and in between courses was Rosa's (Claudia's cousin) risotto with radicchio. I wasn't able to eat for two days it seemed—but I managed to eat all the leftovers sent home with me.) Bello was out of town for the soiree.

---

[26] *Frazione.* District or neighborhood
[27] *Parmigiana.* Parmesan

I must go let the birds out... more tomorrow. I promise this will eventually be sent to you. JJ

Last installment—I will send this out today!

It is the 8th of May... I just realized—my mother and Claudia's mother share the same birth date. I wonder if it is the same year...?

Well, the chickens have flown the coop—as in liberated themselves from the coop. It took a few grueling days to get Rocket to just calm down around them and now they are becoming steadfast friends, although he loves it when it is time to herd them into their coop at sunset. He actually lives for that time of the day. He practices herding them all day, actually. Jackie is still nursing her little cut from the late night tumble to the neighbors—I've since made a barrier to disable her from doing that again—but that didn't stop one of the chickens from checking out the garden below. The lady of the house finally cracked a smile with me— telling me "first your dog in my yard and now your chickens." It was pretty comical. Her husband "Maestro Domenico" came over yesterday (at my request) to show me how to make cement and plaster so I can do repairs around the villa. Here everything is either cemented, nailed, or glued down. I have no idea where I will find the time to cement and plaster though... perhaps this winter. The orto is growing by leaps and bounds. I've had my first eggs, berries, zucchini and basil. Tomatoes are next.... Alberto and I worked the field yesterday—he made posts for the eggplant and tomatoes so they will not fall to the wind and I learned how to remove the weeds with a big hoe and make neat and tidy banks for the plants and water. I've learned a great deal about home repairs, plants, chickens (you would be surprised how smart and perceptive they are and they follow instructions) and seasonal differences that I didn't know coming from California. I think I will compose a list of the 100 things I know now that I didn't know when we arrived. You will no doubt receive that too—one day.

Church bells are ringing in the 7 a.m. hour. Dogs are sleeping, laundry is on, and I think I will take the dogs to Angela's later this morning for some groceries before I'm ensconced here at the villa for the next five days—until Bello returns from the States... he was out the door today at 4:45 *stamattina*[28]. Hence my busy fingers now... espresso at 4:00 a.m. has a way of inspiring one.

Well, there you have it.... Oh, the Marchese family day went well. Bello made the salads and sliced the breads by hand and made the sandwiches. Everyone loved it! Mass was beautiful—the church has similar (but more elaborate) plaster work as does this villa and the mosaic tile we have was done by the same artist Maestro Domenico that did the church years and years ago. One becomes accustomed to 16' ceilings and plaster walls (with layers of details) pretty quickly. I am looking forward to our time back in Santa Barbara and our tiny abode though. And although I love the grounds and the responsibility of the villa—our condo's maintenance sounds pretty dreamy right about now. Come mid-July I'll be really ready to come home. Of this I am certain— Rocket may be a different story though. Jackie will be just fine returning to the safe confines of her Land Rover.

I will soon force myself to send this note to you... bells are ringing the quarter hour...

Oh, the asses have arrived and on a semi-daily bases and the big wall is finally being rebuilt. They have to remove tons of dirt and the old wall and bring in all new materials. It is a huge job. There must be 10 persons and the mules (4) involved in the process. And the Gagliano family is also repairing the wall above this property by removing the top two meters of stone and recapping with new. Another big job.

Baci all... JJ

My Buddy Gennaro Polese – Renaissance Man

Today's offerings: fresh fava beans from two gardens; fish caught this morning in the local waters; home grown wine (two bottles); a jar of *tonno* (tuna)—yes, from the local waters and bottled by the one and the same who made the wine; and fresh doughnuts. It was an incredible

---

[28] *Stamattina.* This morning

fish of some sort—it is long and white and I've forgotten the name. Gennaro Polese (akin to Alberto) was over today for a visit—he had the day off. Gennaro is really cool. *Gli amo come un fratello*[29].

... That was last week. The white fish was fabulous. Fortunately Gennaro gutted it and all I had to do was cut off its head. I figured the least I could do for the creature was eat it being that it gave up its life and all—otherwise I think I would have had vegetables for lunch. Bello refrained from the entire experience. I think it was an eel...

****

Claudia has a new boyfriend... I like him. And apparently she does too. His name is Giuseppe, a.k.a., Peppe. He's no wallflower. Last year I predicted that this would be the year of the boyfriend for Claudia. She's far too special to be single forever. We met Peppe at the really fabulous birthday party for Carmella (Alberto's daughter, who just turned 18, which is cause for major celebration in Italia.) The party... (now, we are flying over Bordeaux) ...was a full on family affair. Cousins and nieces and nephews, sisters and brothers, aunts and uncles, neighbors.... A set table for 50 in the mountains of Agerola—some 3,000 feet straight above our home—by foot the journey takes an hour and by car and hour, but it is best to go by car. Once in Agerola it is another ten minutes up the foothills to the home of Alberto's family. We met and re-met family members and were treated like special guests. I helped administer the incredible *antipasti*[30] that Elisa had prepared of local cheeses and meats, nuts and olives and some kind of jarred vegetables. Then it was off to the pizza *forno* (oven) with Alberto's cousin for an impromptu lesson in pizza tossing and crust crisping.... Both seem much more easy than they are in actuality. And after 50 *pizza margherita* (named after a tribute to Queen Margherita and a Napolitano specialty), it was to the grill for the sausages... then more red wine and finally, the

---

[29] *Gli amo come un fratello.* I love him like a brother.
[30] *Antipasti.* Appetizers. Considered a prelude to any Italian meal where culinary foreplay is paramount.

Karaoke with Alberto and me and another friend for some rendition in something italiano. And after that, it was time to go. Understandably.

Cycles of Life

The *orto* is growing at an almost unimaginable rate for a beach city guy to grasp. Two weeks in the life span of a tomato or *basilico* plant represents quite a bit of their existence and they waste no time in expressing themselves. I am finding all of nature to be that way. It is like each creature and plant and being is saying "hey, I'm here for such a short time and I'm going to do my very best to get noticed." I was in the lower terrace (the abandoned terrace) and I mistakenly decapitated the most fabulous hollyhock flower that was reaching 6 feet tall—the very plant that was the impetus of my tackling that particular terrace. It made me really sad. I had to stop work for a while and think about that plant... although it reseeds itself every year it was now deprived of that process this year and wasn't able to be the star in the garden that it was—but is now food for the worms.... The cycle of life on a truly mundane yet profound level—depending on if you are that worm or not...

Oh, I had a great connection with Luca— something was off two weeks ago, I don't know what, but this week we had a great connection and Luca brought me a bag of corn to plant so that the chickens will have corn to eat for the winter—as opposed to getting corn meal from the feed store. How practical, and green.

Marcello

...and finally, a new stove for the villa—ours was 30 years old, according to Marcello. Marcello is popular and it took six days to have the delivery finally happen—he called me 20 minutes before he wanted to arrive, but I said of course! Now I can cook on more then two burners and actually close the oven door without having to arm-wrestle it to the ground. We will stop by some time and pay for it... details, details... right?

Baci,

JJ

... And how times flies by. It is now the 10th or so of June and it seems like an entire lifetime has gone by since I last sent you a note. I've learned as of late that nothing is ever the same. Everything is slowly evolving and reverting back from where it came. You really notice this with nature. In Santa Barbara, one's garden grows all year and we tend to forget that that isn't reality for the majority of the world. Here, nature has all four seasons to work through and each passing day is but a part of the fleeting season. I've noticed this first with waning zucchini and then with the similarly waning *gelso* [31]tree. It is like there is a rush to become a full-blown productive plant in all its glory and the moment that point is reached there is a noticeable retreat. It is amazing. I've been collecting, bottling, jarring, canning (not really canning) as fast as I can, but there is always something on the cusp. Today it is the capers. Capers, apparently, must be picked when the berries are medium sized, well before they flower and not when they are the size that we Americans purchase at the store – and on the stem! The foliage and berries (*sans* stem) are then to be placed in salt for four days and rotated twice daily. Afterwards, one should have preserved capers. Michele, who is one of the wall builders recapping the HUGE wall that runs the entire length of the villa's grounds and holds up the world behind us, lives in Agerola near Alberto and is the one who gave me the caper recipe. I've come to really appreciate the people of Agerola. Without them there would be nobody to feed and work the Amalfi Coast. Also, today, I am wanting to make another batch of *gelso* marmalade because the berries are at the peak today. I made wonderful pesto (ten cups) day before yesterday with the *basilico* from our *orto* (which is getting a fine reputation even here amongst true farmers) and today I must prune the Ballarati/Florena *basilico* down below because it is becoming tree-like and all the leaves below the canopy can not receive the sun's rays. I have to let the chickens out shortly (after my second coffee) and pick the zucchini for the day. Then I should check in on the other wall builders totally replacing the huge wall that

---

[31] *Gelso.* Mulberry

completely fell down on the other side of the property—next to my *orto*. They have to excavate tons and tons of fabulous soil for the new wall (they are replacing it with cement) and I am the lucky recipient of all the new dirt. My terraced *orto* is becoming a huge mesa.

Our New Frigo

Big news: we now have a refrigerator that doesn't require one to change the towel under the vegetable bin because of excess condensation. And one that is as tall as I am. It is wonderful. I think I mentioned our new stove in an earlier note? It came two weeks ago, so perhaps I haven't made mention of it yet. Both appliances arrived without ever a mention of actually paying for them. Here, it is assumed that you will come down to the shop and pay for the new items when convenient. And they only take cash. Everyone accepts credit cards but their credit card machines are NEVER working. Just like the ATMs, apparently. Next purchase will either be a new faucet for the sink or an entirely new sink all together. Ours is always scalding you.... You see, there is the HOT valve—hot, as in *boiling*, and there is the cold spout. You have to do the regulating. It isn't pretty and it is quite painful. We are creating a very workable *cucina*[32]!

Luca, Alberto, and Chicken Advice

What else.... There is so much to tell... Luca from above (his family is doing both wall repairs and is building the B&B next door) brought me corn seeds last month and showed me how to plant corn. I bet you didn't know that you plant corn (and peas) three kernels per hole—well, you do. I now have a corn patch. It is feed for the chickens for the fall and winter months. And it is my tomatoes that are garnishing the fine reputation... Alberto created the MOST attractive system of poles (you have to have poles and supports for your produce due to winds here) and supports for our produce by using the old and fabulous wood supports for the old grape vineyard that preceded my *orto*. While others use bamboo, we use aged wooden branches. Due to all the wall works going on, there is an incredible amount of individuals who traverse the

---

[32] *Cucina*. Kitchen. Arguably the most significant room in the house.

back *orto* (but never venture to the villa's grounds unless invited), so I have LOADS of advice given to me about everything. Did you know that you shouldn't give your chickens too much dried bread because they will eat their shells? Sounds plausible... but... that came from Tina's mom (you don't know Tina), Maria. According to Luca, give your chickens mussel shells (they have a fish market in town, too) and your chickens will refrain from eating their eggs.... Don't feed chickens at night—they can't see the food and it attracts mice—or worse... Have a rooster, don't have a rooster... the list goes on and on—and that's just about the chickens. Our chickens roam the villa grounds and follow me around like a pack of dogs.... This would include Rocket and Jackie too. It is funny beyond words. You know me, so you can only imagine what a complete kick that I get out of having the entire menagerie running and trying to keep up with me.... poor Jackie though—she's good for about 20 minutes of outdoor play time before she is ready to head back indoors for a siesta.

****

And Jackie is off her painkillers!!! Her eyes are getting worse though. She manages the grounds by memory and I keep all the dirt paths rock free and swept for her. It is like Braille for her. It really works.

What else is new...? I realize that I've been here for four months and have yet to go to the sea... yet to lunch in Positano, yet to climb the mountain behind us and yet to do a great many of the things that we cherish about this place. Oh well, perhaps this month. I always say that though.

Tina's Mom

I must go let out the chickens... I'm bringing Maria (Tina's mother) today's fresh eggs and some zucchini and homemade pesto and marmalade. She is great—TOTALLY OUT THERE! I love her. She's really Italian—arms flying when she speaks and has something to say about everything—most often when you are not in the room... I can only imagine what she says about me. But that is part of her 80-year charm. She makes a really mean espresso, due to the fact that she never actually washes out the espresso maker—just adds more espresso... she lives about 100 yards directly across from our garden but there is a large piece of land between us, so you have to go down to the street (56 steps), up the road 100 yards and then up her stairs (151 according to Maria).

Suddenly it is eerily quite outside. I better go investigate. Second coffee: finished.

June in Italia...

June 23rd... Church bells are ringing, reminding me of the already seemingly fleeting day—and it is only 7:45 in mattina[33]. *Caffè numero due in mano[34]... Rockettino just bolted in from outside— I heard him barking outside just now— it was his "good morning—remember me!" bark to all the workmen who began their work day here at the villa about an hour ago. Well, they arrived about an hour ago. It takes the guys an hour or two to really get their pace going and then it is time for the mid-morning break—then they really get working, then it is suddenly the lunch hour and before you know it, it is four in the afternoon. Needless to say that projects take an awful long time to complete around here—almost as long as they do to plan. But the outcome is nothing short of pure perfection. You can apply this theory to most any Italian and Italian trade. This observation is made with the uttermost of respect for Italians—as a whole.*

This is going to be one of those epic notes I feel that many of you read in parts...

Where to begin? For certain, the villa is beyond great—she has high ceilings of 18 feet and finished of in truly ornate plaster of a long-gone age... The doors are thick and of old-growth wood and the doorways are about 1-meter deep. And the 100-year-old eclectic flooring is in itself its own book.... Over the last century it has been divided into about seven

---

[33] *In mattina.* In the morning. Mattina – a term used solely for the morning hours prior to 10:00 am

[34] *Caffè numero due in mano.* Coffee Number 2 in hand

abodes, including ours. Here we have what I call the Montebello family—those that have been here for years and when they come together at this place, they also come together at the dining table. It is really special. Everyone has their own lives and outside worlds but there is also a bond with those others that share the space. Catarina is the quintessential Toscana woman, being followed closely for the reining title by her daughter, Benedetta, or Bendi. (Women from Toscana have an uncanny ability to take the most basic item and make it look like a million euro—say a bowl of lemons… or, take three ingredients from the cupboard or garden and make a feast. But don't expect them to waste a thing or wait around for any compliments for they are far too pragmatic for accolades, considered a triviality when you know you're dead on—as they do. If you recall, Catarina and Bendi had Hannah and me over for *Pasquale*[35] this spring. And then there is Massimo—Catarina's husband. Imagine a 6-foot 4-inch tall and very handsome Italian named Massimo with a commanding voice and contagious smile and then square it and double that and you begin to get the picture of Massimo. Rockettino simply adores Massimo—for he allows Rockettino not only in their house and kitchen but in the trash bin as well. You don't tell Massimo no. You just don't. He reminds me of an Italian James Bond. All the Ballarati boys do. Then there is Michele. He and Heidi (she's from Honduras) were married three years ago and we were present for the ceremony in Toscana and the reception at the family farm afterwards… that is its own tale… but think long table for 150 where couples were split up and an impromptu football (soccer) match mid afternoon—and dancing around midnight and you begin to get the feel… they've a daughter named Sofia who is now about two… And also there is Bendi's man—Federico Florena. They wed just two years ago and have Lisa, who is almost two. Feddy (his nickname) is an architect in Napoli—Michele and Heidi live in *Londra* (London). Catarina's mother was the first to rent here almost 50 plus years ago and the entire family thinks as Montebello as their second home… My second room used to be theirs and my second bath as well—that was before Mario (our Patron owner)

---

[35] *Pasquale*. Easter. Besides representing the resurrection of Christ, *Pasquale* represents the start of a new tourist season on the coast.

walled up their staircase three winters ago to accommodate the growing Marchese tribe.

Upstairs: on our level. All the rooms on the upper floor (ours) originally opened one to the next much like the Hall of Mirrors in Versailles, and created the most fantastic long gallery that ran the entire length of the villa. Ideally one should be able to go from one end of the villa to the other and never lose the sea view—ideally.

Sweet and Sour Aubergine Caponata all Siciliana by Caterina

Serves 6

3 medium eggplants (melanzane italiane [long, not round])
2 large sweet peppers (red or yellow)
3 medium sweet onions (Maui, sweet not strong)
1 garlic clove (flavor only, remove before serving)
3 tablespoons diced celery
1 bunch fresh basil
3 tablespoons toasted or fried-and-dried pinenuts
3 tablespoons raisins or sultanas
2 tablespoons brown sugar
½ cup white wine vinegar
2 tablespoons chopped fresh mint
4 ripe medium tomatoes
vegetable oil to fry eggplant
4 tablespoons olive oil to sauté other vegetables

Eggplants: dice, fry, and dry.

Dice all other vegetables (and basil) and sauté with olive oil over a brisk fire (garlic not diced, it is removed later). After vegetables begin to curl (about 5 minutes), add sugar, vinegar, and raisins. Let vinegar evaporate 3 to 4 minutes, then cook over low flame for 20 minutes (until peppers soften). Add fried eggplant, leave on flame for 2 to 5 minutes.

Serve on a platter with fresh mint and pinenuts sprinkled on top (don't serve too hot, can be served cold).

40

****

Lady Marchese and her son surprised me yesterday with a visit. I surprised *them* with the new stove, refrigerator, and custom-made patio cushions. I love being the bigger surprise! I sent them off four hours later with fruit, vegetables, and eggs from their villa.... Speaking of which... I can hear a chicken in the distance making her "I just laid an egg" cry.... Time to let the girls out, I guess.

Stamattina (This Morning)

Suddenly it is 10:30... I've been up in the orto watering.... Now I know exactly why people that live in the country have so many children. It is very pragmatic, actually. I've come to recently realize that it is of physical impossibility to keep this place up alone, Bello does a great deal as well. I've decided this morning to not try. You wouldn't believe the calluses that I've on my feet. Weeds are going to have to be tolerated for the duration if I am going to have a moment to actually enjoy myself— and to getting around to making another batch of pesto for the freezer and some fig preserves for this fall and winter. I still have yet to get to the ripening capers on the great wall—that may have to be a year *due progetto*[36].

The *orto* is on the cusp of finishing the zucchini and the tomatoes and *melanzane* (eggplants) are about to yield baskets and bushels daily. I hope somebody does something with all of this next month and in August when we are away... but I can only control what is reasonable... controlling this garden while 6,000 miles away is not reasonable.

I am boycotting the market this week (there is ample milk and bubbly in the house) and am only going to eat what I can pick for the next couple of days... kind of a game. Bello is in the Caribbean this week so I have to find creative ways to pass the time... pasta is the exception though.... Here, pasta is its own food group.

---

[36] *Year due progetto.* Italianglish for "Year 2 project."

Pasta recipe: Zucchini and spring onions by Giuliana

Chop a couple of spring onions (white) and thinly slice numerous small baby zucchini and cook in a non-stick pan with olive oil until crisp and tender—about 20 minutes

Boil heavily salted water for the pasta—add pasta—cook al dente and SAVE THE WATER—keep the pasta in the water...

Add some of the pasta water and some freshly grated Parmesan to the vegetable mix.... Warm and keep stirring... add an egg and stir.... Add some more water... some pasta... another egg, stir... add more cheese... some more pasta, water, cheese.... Keep stirring.... And eventually the pasta has all been married with the vegetables and the result is the most fabulous pasta dish for this particular moment of the vegetable season.

Next week it will be ALL about tomatoes and eggplants... and zucchini and onions will be a thing of the past.... I've made this particular pasta for Bello 15 of the past 20 days—seriously. He loves it, and I've gotten the recipe down. Believe me. I will make a last batch of the zucchini pasta tomorrow and freeze it for later this fall when there are no zucchini or spring onions at the market... off to the garden for some more watering—this time the formal garden where it is shaded all morning and into the mid afternoon. But first—to the fig tree for the figs are as black as charcoal and they will soon start dropping to the ground—and that I consider tragic. .... 36 hours (or so later)... the figs waited another day and it was well worth it and my boycott of the market (delivery) was a total farce—for tomorrow I am making a great batch of pesto. I've said it before: a lot can happen around here in 24 hours—let alone 36 hours.

Since the arrival and departure of the *famiglia*[37] Marchese, there has been a minor trash issue with the community and the villa—some of the friends of friends placed their garbage in the wrong place on the wrong day in the wrong-colored bag—seriously –and seriously because to do so is considered "*different refuse on or in the wrong-colored bag on the*

---

[37] *Famiglia*. Family

wrong day." It is both criminal and as quite understandable, on occasion, in the village. I spotted the errant garbage and retrieved it yesterday, but apparently, that wasn't fast enough because Claudia received a call about it today. Absolutely nothing goes unnoticed on the Amalfi Coast—nothing. That is why having this great big spread is so special—I can roam about and do my thing and mostly go unnoticed by the community in general. Don't think I'm being conceited—I'm not and it's true—everyone gets noticed here and everyone notices everything. I meet people in Cuore del Mare and they can't believe that I've been here an entire year almost without them ever seeing me. I rather like that at the moment.

I was accused recently of not really being here and writing these missives from the comfort of the Beverly Hills Hotel's bungalows for future screenplay... I assure that's not the case—yet. I do have the calluses to prove my actual intent. I will however attach an appropriate photo to add further reassurance that I'm not living it up in the 90210.

The Bells of Montebello

Bells are ringing midnight. I'm going to bed. More tomorrow. Baci, JJ

... God is it hot-- even now, at 6 *in mattina*. It is impossible to *dormire*[38]—impossible. In addition to Homer writing his tales from these parts after spending a winter here, I think Dante must have gotten the idea of "Inferno" from spending a summer here as well. I don't know how many of your actually read Dante's *Inferno*—I'm not saying that this is by any means a purgatory—it's just hot. Still utterly beautiful— just bloody hot. The air isn't moving. Capri—where's Capri? I can barely make out Positano. I'm determined to get to the *orto* this morning and give my fledgling tomatoes and eggplants a drink before the sun comes over the rise.... First my coffee... bells are ringing the ¼ hour—time is fleeting.

****

---

[38] *Dormire*. To sleep

June 29th... and the season (for us) is drawing to an end. And I am rather excited, to tell the truth. By now, you all know how much and why I love it here so much, but there is something awfully alluring about returning to Santa Barbara in July—not to bloody hot (like it is rapidly becoming here) and all the comforts that we've come to appreciate and do without here—like a car, or a cloths dryer—although I've come to find that neither are crucial to one's existence. (Jackie may beg to differ on the car detail.)

Our second coffee is almost finished slowly brewing and my bello is letting the birds out and collecting their eggs and today's zucchini. Our 12 zucchini plants have been pumping out vegetables for about two months now—and the eggplants are about to rapidly overtake them in production. And how about the 60 (or so) tomato plants... what was I thinking in the early spring—I don't know. It is a shame that we have to go—although Bello is considering not leaving.... Really. So, there may be a July in Italia to follow.... I can't see us spending an August here on the coast though—too hot, too many Italians, not enough beach chairs, parking spaces, or cool breezes to suffice. No, August is simply for Italians living in Italia in my book—it is their month off and they should get the perks (and headaches and hassles).

$$\ast\ast\ast\ast\ast\ast\ast\ast\ast\ast\ast\ast\ast\ast\ast\ast\ast\ast$$

My bello is back in from the orto—overwhelmed with the sheer volume of coming eggplant and pomodoro. He just asked: "How do you prepare eggplants for Siciliana[39]?"... "What are you going to do with all these eggs?"... and out the door he goes.... He's the best! Bells are ringing 10 a.m.—time to run. There is much to do just in sweeping my walkways and terraces before we leave for the beach. Thank God that it rained last night and I'm free from watering duties for the day (or possibly two).

$$\ast\ast\ast\ast\ast\ast\ast\ast\ast\ast\ast\ast\ast\ast\ast\ast\ast\ast$$

---

[39] He is referring to the *caponata* that Caterina made for us the first night we met. An unexpected but wholly amazing sweet-and-sour is best way to describe it.

… Big news (I briefly mentioned this above)—the new recycling system for the entire coast has been put into place. There is a special colored bag for each different type of recyclable and each bag has a different day of pickup. *Multo complicato per tutte persone, pero importante. Per me no problema pero io un grande villa and muti stanze e deposito per spazzatura. Pero per* those other *persone in Cuore del Mare* who are not so *fortunato*—it is a drama. Change does not come easily here. But things are changing—even here in the South.

… That was yesterday and this morning is about a carbon copy of the above. Bello is about to return from letting the birds out and he'll have something to say about the eggs, eggplant, and tomatoes…. Last night we harvested the first pail of *pomodorini*—the little cherry tomatoes. Tonight I will be making something melanzane…

May and June are the best months for a visit here… (this would be a hint). But I do believe that next year's guest calendar is going to fill rapidly… another hint.

… Bello is back… he fears that we have too much eggplant… he's going to make a deal with Angella (Luca's mom—she has the *alimentari* we favor).

Baci e abbracci,

JJ

P.S. Second coffee is being prepared by my bello—and last night we had Stefano and Giuliana over for dinner with their friend Tina, who lives up in the Tyrolean Alps above Venice. It was the zucchini and spring onion dish for dinner by request from Stefano and Bello—again.

We were able to catch up and plan next year's meet-ups – we've been invited yet again to Apulia and next year we must take them up on their heartfelt offer…

I left Giuliana with a huge stash of this past season's *marmalata*[40] and jam and she promised to make sure that they were distributed – nobody likes last year's preserves (right?) because there is bound to be more the following year. God, I really love this place...

Until next year, Montebello,

James

---

[40] *Marmalata*. Marmalade

Year 2 Living Abroad
5. March in Italia...

Well, I just sat through an entire reading of last year's escapades and, quite frankly, nothing seems to have really changed all that much and I hope you don't find this a boring year. I personally take great solace in the status quo, for what could be better then wanting nothing more than what already exists? Really. Bello may quote me later on this—but he doesn't read my travel notes, so the chances of that are slim.

It is now almost midnight in California and around 8 *in mattina* here. My bello is in Santa Barbara and returns to the Coast Monday morning. He left well before the crack of dawn on Tuesday bound for the Caribbean for a quick meeting and later today he flies from L.A. to Washington for a work meeting and a visit with his family, and then back home here early Monday morning. He claims that this will be the longest trip of the year, but that, too, is the same story as last year... we'll see about that as the weeks and months tick by...

Alone at the Villa with My Aging Dog

Being alone at the villa is interesting to the point of weirdness after several days. I'm not really alone of course—hence the 4 a.m. wakeup call from Jackie Chan, who, when she wakes, must be taken somewhere to pee immediately or she will simply take matters into her own paws. After their brief excursion outside, Rocket was right back to bed, but Jackie did her pacing about the bedroom and salotto[41] for about three hours and finally went back to bed—too late for me though with two espresso already under my belt... so I'll chat a bit...

---

[41] *Salotto.* Living room. *Salotto* is more a designation of a somewhat "common" personal living space or receiving space, generally a term reserved for a larger domicile.

Speaking of Jackie Chan, she is really getting up there in age. This year she celebrated her 15th birthday, although I don't think she is counting. She is basically blind now and has a constantly tearing eye that requires dutiful swabbing, but she is all right with it—I think it is a relief to her plus it is always followed up with a treat. She seems to have become resolved to being all right with the whole aging thing. She allows me to bring her to and from where she needs to go and relies on me to make sure she doesn't kill herself on an almost daily basis. Three days ago, we were out on the main walk in the formal garden doing her back and forth, back and forth pattern of two meters forwards and one meter back and suddenly she was nowhere in sight... I ran to house, past the house—back to the main garden and instinctively looked over the great wall and there she was below—all right, but obviously very perplexed and confused as she never saw the fall coming (thankfully) and was cushioned by landing on years of garden debris we throw over the wall from the upper garden. We dodged a huge bullet that time. The fall was double what she pulled off last year at Maestro Domenico's garden— double. We are talking 20 plus feet. Not even a scratch. She has to be physically watched at all times outside or pinned along a walkway as I do for she still likes to walk in the garden several times a day. She loves waking up in the morning and loves it when Rocket joins her on her bed for cuddling and loves to eat and be with the three of us. For the moment all is tutto posto *with the* Princepessa[42].

Rocket

Rockettino could not be happier back in his garden where, according to him, he rules the roost. He is particularly interested in the cats that have made the grounds theirs as well during his absence and he is righting that wrong quickly. However there is a big tabby that isn't backing down so easily and Rocky has had his first moment of defiance from a feline. He was shocked and got a swat on the face to boot. "Don't mess with big tabby cats" is the lesson learned here. He follows me everywhere in the garden and if I am outside all day, so is he. He takes his naps when

---

[42] *Principessa*. Princess. A gentile term often reflecting an endearing fondness (*not* condescension).

he can—sometimes he simply closes his eyes and falls over right in the garden when the need to sleep is stronger then his willpower to play. He's a dedicated dog and watches Jackie in the garden as best he can. Being that Jackie cannot see, she is very often mistaking his ear for a treat or him for a pillow on her bed, yet he is always a good sport about it and doesn't hold it against her. I think he gets it that she is just really old.

The wind is howling like I've never seen or heard it howl before, but I'm sure it has been worse. I spotted a dusting of snow on the mountaintops from last night—needless to say it is cold here today. Last week was the first nice week the Coast has seen since October from what EVERYONE has told us, so we feel pretty fortunate to have had the sunshine for so many days in a row. Back to reality now I guess—for this wind and rain and hail could be the case for several more weeks to come...

✶✶✶✶✶✶✶✶✶✶✶✶✶✶✶✶✶✶

Remember our best friend Claudia? She and I went to Positano for a little giro[43] day before yesterday in the afternoon. I've come to realize that there is no place like Positano in the summer and no place like Santa Barbara in the winter. She and I had a great time. I had two gelati[44]—she had one. There is nothing like gelato in Positano—even if it is cold out. Perhaps she and I will go somewhere today—although our options are limited due to the road closure that is splitting the coast in two this spring—all due to a big boulder that is precariously dangling over the only coastal road at the end of one of the *gallerie*[45] (tunnels). It is like having the 101 closed between Santa Barbara and Montecito without any other route except by foot to reach the other. It is so old-world Amalfi Coast. So, perhaps it is Positano again—I could use a

---

[43] *Giro.* Tour
[44] *Gelati.* Plural of *gelato.* The Italian frozen treat that approximates ice cream but is one thousand times better.
[45] *Gallerie.* Tunnels, galleries. Along the costierra, development of *gallerie* were essential components of road development given that the near-vertical topography that plunges into the sea. The *gallerie* also serve as road landmarks – "...just before the fourth tunnel..."

49

Herald-Tribune and our village's *giornali*[46] isn't stocking the *Herald* just yet.

Almost nine *in mattina*... now Jackie sleeps... A hot shower seems in order... ciao for now...

Blessings, Absurdities, and the Status Quo

... And here we are, quickly approaching the last couple of days of March... I got up early this morning because Jackie Chan slept through the entire night, so I did as well. Bello is still sleeping, or at least keeping really still with hopes that his coffee will mysteriously present itself. I'm guessing it will. I've already had one cup with a hot bath and another will be just what is needed to get me out to the garden early. I have to relocate my orto this year and that is no easy task, for I have already cleared and prepped the entire area for this year's garden and ordered the plants. Vivianna is going to have big party to promote her Spanish/Italian language school here NEXT June and Lui and Damiana are going to get married NEXT August and have their reception here— both events are to be held in what was the orto. My gut tells me that the orto had its one grand year in the best spot on the property and now it is time to make adjustments for the future. I know what you are thinking and it is what it is... I'm fine with it. I have, however, refrained from amending my plant order and am going to accommodate the move with pleasure. These things (like all others) have a way of working themselves out in the end and all we have to do is manage to stay out of the way when the universe is dictating things. So I shall, as best I can. The plan is to level the acre and put in a lawn and sprinkler system. (The word sprinkler is a word that does not exist in the Italian language because it is impossible for Italians to pronounce for one, and secondly because they don't have sprinkler systems here because they don't have lawns here.) But after careful reasoning about the actual difficulty and expense of that idea, we are back to the terrace approach that I currently have employed in the orto (the old orto) and we will expand on the terraces to create larger paddocks for the parties next year. What I

---

[46] *Giornali.* Newsstand

*am getting myself into is still yet to be fully determined, however I am
certain you will be hearing more about this in the coming months... but
this year's "new orto" will be stunning. Oh, we are also relocating the
chicken coop because that has to be torn apart and refashioned into the
bar for the parties. I'm not complaining though. I don't complain out
load anymore—status quo and all. Rockettino wants out to respond to a
barking friend and Jackie would like to go walk some path laps... and
Bello still sleeps* ☺

The Nature of Human Nature

I'm out to the garden—*senza la secondo caffè*[47]—a first. Today is the
last Saturday of the month. Next week everyone puts away their black,
brown, and grey clothing and suddenly it will be spring on the
Costierra[48]. The actual weather here dictates less to one's attire then
does the actual date on the calendar. The nature of human nature
seems somewhat predictable.

I have a sneaking suspicion that all of my *orto* plants will be arriving
today from *Posiflora*[49]: 3 types of tomatoes (15 each), loads of
eggplant, thyme (although it grows like a weed here I ordered a lovely
variegated (6 *in fatto*[50]), loads of *basilico* and, our favorite, zucchini. And
the chickens should be making their trek down from Agerola any day
now—provided that the *galleria* (that is tunnel, not mall) on the other
side of Cuore del Mare is open... the hanging question here on the
Coast.... you see—from what I am told, there is not merely one—but a
rather large set of boulders hanging over the lip of the *galleria* entrance,
and while the rocks are being excavated all *Costierra* traffic is halted—
divided. And to get from one to the other you have to park your car and
walk around a hill, down to the sea and up the other side of the hill to
get to the other side of the 40-yard long tunnel. As you can imagine, it is

---

[47] Senza la seconda caffè. Without the second coffee
[48] *Costierra*. Understood as reference to the Amalfi Coast
[49] *Posiflora*. One of the garden shops on the main road through Positano –
both are on the "mountain" side of the road, occupying former caverns and
spilling their plants and garden accouterment onto the roadway.
[50] *In fatto*. In fact

the talk of the town. Personally, I think it is a ploy to get the tour bus operators to cease bringing their HUGE coaches down the Amalfi Coast—something that has been in the works and a contested issue on both sides for quite some time. If there is a will then there is always a way here in Italia—it just takes a while to achieve one's goal though, and patience is a major component.

Now how about that second coffee... Baci e abbracci, James, et al.

Year 2 Living Abroad

6. April in Italia

Just a quick note before the day and then the week pass by without my checking in...There was a *terremoto*[51] in Italia yesterday. We were, fortunately, unscathed however Abruzzi was not nearly so lucky. I didn't actually hear about it until several of you sent emails inquiring about our wellbeing—thank you. Italy is a very resilient country. There is probably a rather short list of countries that have had more rivals pilfer and pillage their land over time then this place and it has certainly had (and recovered from) its fair share of natural disasters. And what will come out of the ruins of yesterday's disaster will no doubt be a better place with lessons learned and the Italians will continue trotting on. It's tough retrofitting an entire country in preparation for these things when everything around you is ancient, historically significant, and aesthetically perfect. With all this talent and panache for presentation you would think Italian news would be a bit more progressive— beautiful blondes (there are no real blondes here) for anchor persons and retired military personnel (in uniform) as the trusted weathermen— weather outranks actual news here in Italia—hence the uniforms.

****

Today Claudia phoned and asked if I would like to accompany her and Raimondo (and his two true blonde labs that Rocky knows and likes), plus another friend (from San Diego), to go for a hike to the Nocelle[52]. I / we jumped at the chance and I am working Jackie Chan out as I type so she will snooze the entire time we are out. She is doing her "laps" along

---

[51] *Terremoto.* Earthquake
[52] *Nocelle* is a small village hanging on the slopes above Positano and Montepertuso. Up until a few years ago, the only access to Nocelle was by stairs from Montepertuso or as a hiker on the Path of the Gods. The "road" now links Positano and Montepertuso to a large parking lot at the foot of the village. Bus service is even available now.

the *galleria* out the front door. It is fully enclosed and she has almost zero chance of hurting herself—with the exception when she is turning around and she whacks her head on the rock wall that guides her. She is a trooper though and I can tell when she has had enough—usually after about 90 minutes of walking and turning and trotting up the 9 stairs that lead to the *galleria* will do the trick to guarantee you about 3-4 hours of sound sleeping. Yesterday she decided to let herself in the front door by pushing the screen door open with her nose and she proceeded to enter the landing and immediately walk through two huge marble mortar and pestles that I use (apparently unsuccessfully) as blocks to prevent this from happening and right onto the vestibule (which is my second line of defense) where I was able to rescue her from. Sometimes, the best-laid plans fail. This time without too much fallout—so to speak.

My First "Epic" Marmalade-Making Session

Last night was "an epic marmalade-making session." Epic. What the heck was I thinking picking 40 oranges and 40 lemons at once for making jam...? It's not the easiest thing to do—particularly for the first time. But Giuliana gave me a tutorial day before yesterday, so I felt prepared. And I figured it was only cooked fruit and sugar. Firstly, you have to poke loads of fork holes into the fruit (without puncturing the actual fruit but only the skin) and then proceed to soak the fruit in water for 24 hours, changing the water several times (although I cheated and changed the water only twice without problem) before you slice the fruit the following day. And if you've ever eaten marmalade, then you know that it consists of very small and uniform pieces of skin that have to be separated from all seeds and the white, bitter-tasting skin surrounding the actual fruit. It is tedious. Tedious. Fortunately, for me, Alberto and Alicia and Matino arrived (with rototiller in tow) to work on preparing the new party terrace (my old orto) for the upcoming Marchese family events to take place next year. Well, I commandeered Alicia from the less glamorous task in the garden and she helped me whip out the oranges in no time at all. No time at all compared to the hours that the lemon prep took me. Well, the outcome was superb, from what I have tasted so far.... But from point A to point B is a long journey. After three pots cooking on the stove for four hours or so, four hours of fruit prep, a day of soaking, and the two days of weeding just to make my way to the old citrus trees to gather their fruit it was still totally worth it not to have all that fruit simply rot on the ground. And these aren't just any citrus trees (you knew that though)... these are 40-plus-year-old grafted orange and lemon trees. Half the tree is lemon and the other half orange. These trees are on the lower terrace jointly held by the extended Marchese family that is part of the land that has the two fig trees I love so much, and the grumpy uncle that watches me like a hawk to make sure that I don't throw out garden clippings (tree branches and the like) or pick the fruit down below—both of which I do and have no intention on ceasing. The fig trees were on their last legs several years back, but with considerable annual cleaning and pruning both trees are accessible and thriving again. The white fig tree was almost covered with a poison ivy-like plant a few years ago and I have completely pulled that plant (and its awful root system) back about 20 feet from the tree. So you see, I earn the fruit that I harvest. The lower path is the first path that I used 12 years ago, before one could even access the upper garden entry that we now use. It was the path everyone used before the big conflict between Mario and his two sister's husbands about them pitching in to help cover the cost of maintaining the path. They refused and the gate was locked. And that was that. We all then started using the upper gate and I started gardening up there as well.... It is nice to have the lower path accessible again, though even if it is only from our side (although those of us that live here know exactly how to open the old lock with your little finger by slipping it in the backside of the lock, but we will keep that a secret). It really IS a secret garden. And the old roses are as special as the old citrus. Did you know that the older the tree the better it is for making marmalade because the really old trees produce fruit with thick skins and lousy fruit—perfect for marmalade. The awful "ick" plant with the thorns was completely engrossed in the fruit trees and the roses a couple of years ago and each spring I tackle a bit more of it. It is almost back to its original bush and when I reach it I will burn it. That I know for certain.

****

I better go check on Jackie Chan—it's been a bit too quiet out there... she's fine. I'm making a second cup of coffee and then I will start making my vegetable sauce so I have something to eat tonight. Garlic, onions, red and yellow peppers, and zucchini all sautéed together with fresh tomatoes and good jarred tomatoes and three hours later, voila. I'll freeze half. And my fridge-and-freezer finally no longer smells of everything that was in it that rotted when the power was out for an extended period this past winter. It was awful. There was something with fish involved that was in the freezer that was the worst—although rotten pesto is pretty bad, too.

People's Court Italia—there is no worse television. *Secondo caffè in mano—tutto posto. Arrivederci.* Giacomo.

****

... And how the month flies by... it is now the 15th of April and so much has happened at the same time that all is really much the same. That is the beauty of irony.

Easter in Italia

Back to the villa—the wisteria on the great terrace was in all its glory these past two weeks. I mentioned it last year, as it represents the temperament of nature really, as I have come to recognize it—fleeting. It reminds me of a quote from Emerson I read this morning about making one's spare moments count because once they are gone they are never retrieved again. So true. I hope that you all make this day, this moment count. I guess you are if your reading this now and not doing one of the countless important things on all of your lists—I thank you very much for that. Seriously. The wisteria's timing could not have been better, for it was perfect for the Easter weekend. And Easter is a weekend affair in Europe. There is, of course, Easter day but, there is also Easter Monday—almost as coveted for it is another day off, and we all know how much Europeans cherish extra days off—particularly when it is in the spring and after a long winter of being indoors and wearing way too many layers of clothing. I kind of get their sentiment now after spending a couple of early springs here at the villa. I don't feel the need

56

to experience the full-on winter thing to get the full gist of it though. That is what California is for ☺

＊＊＊＊＊＊＊＊＊＊＊＊＊＊＊＊＊

Well, the Easter weekend was great fun—although the Ballaratis were not here this year and were greatly missed (Michele and Heidi had a little girl whom they named Teresa this winter and Nico and Carolina were visiting from Brazil with their new baby boy so the entire family stayed in Toscana to be with Caterina's mother), I hear that Bendi and Caterina were dreaming of Montebello... we celebrated with Giuliana and Stefano and Generoso and his friends Pier Luigi and Pier Franscesco. I love the names here. I'm the only Giacomo (James) in our village. There are a few in Positano—but there is a St. Giacomo church there, which explains that. We have a St. Gennaro as the father of the village here and the church is named after him, so subsequently there are countless "Gennaro" in our village—we know at least six.... Back to Easter... it all started, of course, with Palm Friday. The village elders (Maestro Domenico and his brother Don Pio, the pastor) arrived at our garden the day before to trim some palm branches to decorate the church and to be used for the great reenactment of Christ caring the cross. The procession ended with a huge mass that was said right in front of the villa, down on the street. Imaging a life-sized Jesus on the cross and 200 people dressed in black, caring candles, and chanting and singing and repeating—it was really something. I put out nice candles on the terrace above and lit our Madonna in the alcove above the main stairs as a symbol of unity—when in Rome... so, that was Friday. Saturday was Saturday and then Easter Sunday, which had all of our group dining on the roof-top terrace taking in the sun and the view of Capri. I set a lovely table and everyone brought or made a rendition of the same dish, *Torta Pasqualina*[53]: artichoke hearts with meat of some sort and peas and parmesan cheese contained in either a bread loaf or in fresh pasta. There were three different versions of it. And all were delicious. And Angela (the owner of our favorite market) made us the

---

[53] *Pasqualina.* Italian Easter Pie.

most beautiful Easter tort as a present—so did Pina—she lives downstairs and takes care of Generoso's and the Ballarati's house—her mother lives above her and they have the *parcheggio*[54] below us as well as the hotel *Tramonto d'Oro* (which her brothers run) downtown, in Montebello. You just never really know who has and owns what around here, unless you hang out for a while. And have I mentioned that it seems that everyone on our hillside is related in one way or another. Cousins, nephews, *zias* and *zios*[55], *nonnas* and *pappas*[56]--which really makes us the outsiders. But we've adapted. Obviously. Back to Easter now... Easter Monday. As if one didn't eat enough the day before, Easter Monday is the national day for eating some more—picnic style. So the plan is that all of Italy goes out for a picnic—all of Italy. You can imagine how popular the Amalfi Coast is for that but you would be surprised that any piece of green grass or low-cut weeds will suffice. Road turnouts for vehicles are quite popular for this purpose. As I said, any patch of green will do, apparently. Not at Villa Marchese though. Stefano and Giuliana had a fantastic assortment of friends come over from Positano, Naples, and Rome and we all picnicked on the roof terrace again. The rule of thumb here is leftovers prevail. (Most decent things here have at least a two-day shelf life.) Needless to say, Tuesday was greeted with much relief for me—with the exception of Bello leaving for Frankfurt that is. Only an overnight trip though to do some brainstorming with the Frankfurt office. He also is working in Naples one day a week (telecommuting as well as going to Naples) with the U.S. Navy that is stationed there. Bello rocks! It's as simple as that. And he's our rock too ☺ He returns today around 4 in the afternoon. It's so chic—he gets picked up and retrieved from the house and heads to interesting ports of call and gets all his work done and still manages to be with us 75% of the week. Not bad, for secret agent work, I suppose...

****

---

[54] *Parcheggio*. Parking area, either enclosed or open air.
[55] *Zias and zios*. Aunts and uncles (kind of...)
[56] *Nonnas and pappas*. Grandmothers and grandfathers (or grandmas and grandpas, depending on the family dynamic...)

Yesterday (Wednesday) I was alone at the villa for the day and roamed around talking to the dogs and listing to music all while gardening, doing the laundry, paying bills on line, and generally having a nice day. I tried to write you but instead sat and listened to the sounds of the village and the coast. By now one can discern just whose vespa is zipping by, or which boat it is traversing back and forth between Positano and Amalfi and which neighbor is walking down the street by the sound of their voice. You know who's working on what project by the sound of the tools and the direction of the sound and the ever-present church bells, which just rang 9:15.

****

I'm thinking that Salvatore, our *idraulico* [57] will return today (he, too, showed up yesterday late afternoon) to investigate our ever-dripping faucet in the kitchen. This is the same faucet I mentioned last year that has separate hot and cold valves so one is constantly burning themselves with the scalding hot water which comes from the water heater directly above the sink. When we arrived this year—in addition to the stinking refrigerator (due to a long power outage during the winter)—we were also greeted by the dripping sink. To get the drip to stop you have to turn off the cold water for half of the house. You want to use the bathroom? Go to the kitchen and turn on the main valve. After six weeks I could take it no longer and I was becoming concerned about turning on and off the main valve so often. You see, if that breaks, we are all screwed. Tile walls are difficult to make repairs behind. And rather costly, too, I would surmise. Everything about an old villa is potentially expensive so you operate with kid gloves in all that you do... careful, that chaise that you are about to sit in is handmade and 80 years old... that dresser—be careful, the inlaid wood may crack if mishandled... the armoire... be really careful, the 7-foot doors are on old hinges... And that is just the bedroom. Poor Pietro, he was here this weekend and on the way out his door he broke the hinge and that will require Luca to come (another Luca). We first met Luca in 2000 when

---

[57] *Idraulico.* Plumber

Bello and I had the misfortune of breaking the wrought iron (very old) door to Generoso's casa and had to have it repaired. Here at the villa if you break it, you fix it. We've fixed many an item. So I am awaiting both Luca and Salvatore today—a 50/50 chance that either will actually come today or later in the week. It isn't that they are unreliable, it is just that other factors may come into play in the interim—like the road to Amalfi being closed unexpectedly or countless other possibilities like me not understanding what I am being told in rapid Italian—which is more so the case, I am certain.

After I am finished updating you, I am going to begin the initial preparations for my third marmalade production. The last batch of sweet orange and a sweet lemon marmalade was good—really good— and totally different from the first round which I did true to tradition and made rather tart. I am about out of oranges below, so this will be the last of the orange marmalade until next year. The best citrus for making marmalade comes from really old trees that produce fruit with thick skin and those trees are down below in the terrace shared by "the uncle" and two aunts— they all live here on the hillside—and I have to be discreet, as to not be seen, for then, a drama will certainly unfold. And my theme for this year: no dramas! I hate of all things being predictable. And last year had plenty of drama. I'll bring grumpy uncle some jam once I've finished with all production from the trees, which should be within the month—there is one lemon tree that still has over 200 pieces of fruit that needs to be picked if the flowers are to develop properly for next year. The trees below are doing great this year because for the past two years, I have been clearing around them and liberating them so that can actually receive sunshine and water—they were covered with vines, the "ick," and morning glory (a stupid name for an invasive plant) and were dying a painfully slow death. Not now, however. Plants react to being taken care of. It's a fact. And something to keep in mind when thinking of creatures higher up in the evolutionary chain. I've come to learn that all living things have an innate will to survive and prosper—think Michael Pollan and his book the *Botany of Desire*! Even worms want to live and regret when they find themselves on the walkway in the sun. I always give them a hand and place them in the wet dirt. A being is a being.

✱✱✱✱✱✱✱✱✱✱✱✱✱✱✱✱✱

Jackie is up for a snack and a garden walk—it is almost 10:15 now…. Rockettino is in his chair awaiting one of us to accompany him outside. We'll both go. According to Alberto, I apparently have planted my *melanzane* incorrectly and have to right that wrong *subito*[58] or they will not be *contento*[59]—who knew? Ciao for now… Baci, JJ

Dangerous Flying Glass and Meeting Our Neighbor Leonardo

April 16… So, the absolute oddest thing occurred here the day before yesterday. And you know that the bar for "oddest bar" has been set pretty high in the past couple of years—with the wacky neighbor and his stealing from us, or the other wacky neighbor and his obsession with the fig tree, or the other conflict with the relatives about the stairs and ingress and egress—well these all pale in comparison to this morning's tale. It all started with Giuliana (who has been spending more time here this year and Stefano has been doing a commute to Naples in the mornings) arriving at my front door with a truly perplexed look on her face. In Italian, she tells me that she isn't going crazy, but that there is glass falling from the sky—or, from the gardens above. Well, I know Giuliana and she is not crazy, which, left the latter as the only possible answer I was willing to acknowledge—because the whole end-of-the-world thing seems a little far fetched to me… anyhow, I immediately go into "villa defensive mode" (as I am prone to do as you are well aware) and head out to the back 40 to investigate. Giuliana and Stefano live on the third level of the villa, which is on the upper most terrace of land, and directly above their garden is the Gagliano garden and some other family we hadn't had the "pleasure" of meeting yet. That was all about to change, for when I arrived at Giuliana's garden there was a huge spear of glass at least ½ a meter sticking in the freshly tilled soil like a Samurai sword. Crazy. Well, I was beside myself. Giuliana explained to

---

[58] *Subito.* Immediately
[59] *Contento.* Content, happy, successful

61

me that she was quietly working amongst her lavender when she heard this loud crashing sound of glass being shattered from above and moment's later shards of glass began raining down from above. That's when she retrieved me. (Giuliana isn't typically at the villa during the week and her area would be somewhat abandoned normally.) I immediately pull the sword of glass from the earth and headed straight up the new 20-foot wall (this is the main wall behind us that was reconstructed last year by the men from Agerola—not to be confused with the other wall that required the mule ramp in the midst of my *orto* as you may recall)—but like a scene straight out of Excalibur I to go to confront whoever... I've learned that in Montebello that if you want someone to come out of hiding for what ever reason and you know that they are there, somewhere, then the best thing to do is simply start yelling at the top of your lungs (in Italian) whatever your point is—and if they are guilty, then they will definitely want to stop your screaming as quickly as possible. It worked, again. After three or four minutes of me telling whomever that I was about to come up *subito* and that they cannot throw glass down at our garden (my prop in hand served to reiterate my point effectively to all the villagers peeking through their window shades).

And, suddenly, a head pops up from behind a *carciofo*[60] plant and I really start yelling then. *"Are tu pazzo*[61]? *Io telephone dei carabinieri subito*[62]."

Well, threatening to bring in the police into anything in Italy is never a desirable position to be in if you're the aggressor. And it is safe to say that the carabinieri would not take glass flying from garden to garden too lightly. So, out of the bush appears this shirtless and obviously drunk man. I had been wondering just how all the old beer bottles were always (year after year after year) amassing themselves on the upper garden terrace in the weeds—I was immediately able to do the math. So Leonardo (his wife is now on the scene up above peering over) tells

---

[60] Carciofo. Artichoke
[61] *Are tu pazzo?* Italianglish for "Are you crazy?"
[62] *Io telefono dei carabinieri subito.* Roughly: I will call the police immediately

me that it wasn't him—so I profusely apologize to both he and his wife and tell them that we had better call the police right away because there is a bandit in their garden throwing glass about the village. He was confused for a moment. Then he confessed. So I really laid into him. Then I found glass in the Gagliano garden. By this point the old guy just wanted the crazy American to shut up. I though I had made my point well enough and he scurried up his hill and started collecting all the glass and bagging it—proudly displaying his cut-up hands from the process—that was the really odd moment that I could have done without—and assuring me that it was over and it would never happen again. (And his every other word was broken English so I know he understood every single word I was saying in my mix-use method.) The funny thing was that although at least 30 neighboring homes from above were in ear- and eyeshot of all of this (and it was high noon when most everyone is home), not a single person was getting involved—that is how it works here—denial mixed with equal parts of denial and denial. It is true. *Strano*[63] it is. I've come to realize that Montebello must resemble the Wild West of America in years past. People here do quite often what they would like and think what's best... Kind of like my attitude with this villa—perhaps that's why were here. So I asked Giuliana about this odd act—throwing glass and all—and she explained that the old guy was simply cleaning out his recycling. I kid you not. This place is almost too much. I can see why there is no other American living here in Montebello. It really is unique. This kind of thing you don't find occurring in Positano or Amalfi—or even in Cuore del Mare (the main part of our village on the other side of the hill)—it is Montebello. This family must have really pissed off some people in years past because the pent up aggression that rears its awful head from time to time with a few of the locals is palpable. But, alas, Leonardo and I ended up shaking hands and saying that all was behind us now.

I will bring Leonardo and his wife up some of my homemade marmalade later this week. I want to know exactly where they live.

---

[63] *Strano.* Strange

Although premature, your receiving April thus far as an update—much more to follow—like I made a nice new *marmalata* yesterday by boiling the lemons first then separating from the juice and fruit and cooking with sugar... and afterwards I shaved my head bald. It's really different. I had an excellent reason... more to follow.

Baci e abbracci.

Shaving Your Head

Ok, so if you have never shaved your head you should really consider it— it is quite liberating. Although the first swipe is a bit of a shock. And have someone help with the back so you don't wind up looking really bizarre. Bello was shocked when he woke from his nap to see my bald head looking back at him from the great terrace. He thought it was someone else at first. As a matter of fact, the entire neighborhood is wondering just who the new guy is working in my garden—the reason for the sudden change of heart regarding my curls was due to the fact that our dear friend is fighting breast cancer and she is beginning to lose her hair and I thought it was appropriate given the situation. I think everyone should shave their head if they even remotely feel inclined. Some people don't have a choice. So, I am bald—what's the big deal, really? I realize what some of you girlfriends of mine must be thinking and I do realize that it is a bit easier for us guys to shave down to the scalp then for you—in theory.

Back to the Orto

Back to the farm.... The chickens arrived the other day—sans one bird though—apparently she didn't make it though the winter due to a leg ailment. It was one of the Pam birds—there were two. All three Rosas returned though—one a bit worse for wear for she is missing some feathers around her neck and is a bit timid this year. Who knows what goes on up in Agerola during the winter.... But the girls seem **very** happy to be back on the Costierra and at Villa Marchese. Rocket was very pleased. But the girls don't fear him this year and standoffs happen almost hourly. Rockettino backs down and the girls realize that there is safety, or at least intimidation, in numbers. We are up to two eggs a day. Rosa and Rosa (with the bad feathers) tend to stay close to the coop and I am guessing that they are the two not laying eggs yet for a nervous chicken does not lay eggs, and if they do they tend to break easily. Rule of thumb in the *orto* is to keep your chickens happy.

Year 2 Living Abroad

7. April in Italia (or so I thought... Part II)

Ciao bello/bella,

I thought it a befitting time to write you—the weather has turned for the worse (actually, that depends on how you interpret it, I guess) and we are in for an early cocktail hour. I purchased a whole chicken this morning (impulse purchase while passing the *macelleria*[64]) and it has been stuffed with onions from the neighbor's garden up above (the same neighbors with the donkeys coming *en masse* later this week through the garden—more, in a minute), and a nice bottle of red wine was just given to me now by Luca (son #3 of the clan above) while Rocket and I were waiting out the rain storm in front of their soon-to-be cantina (the whole house is under total remodel with boulders and dirt and earth and old tile and just construction stuff all over the place for three levels)—it was really nice of him to offer both the tour and the libation. I will depart from the norm of prosecco this evening and have the *vino* with the *pollo* (chicken) tonight—prosecco for now, though...

The Gagliano's Garden

Tomorrow, I will bring the neighbors a lovely box of citrus—the oranges are superb right now—I know this because I was feeling a little low energy this afternoon and I had noticed one of the orange trees in the formal garden (that's what I call it because it is the most manicured portion of the main walk) was heavily laden with oranges in one section, so I climbed it and picked a bag full of fruit and promptly squeezed a couple of pints of juice and drank it *subito* (right away). It was about as perfect as a thing can be. I just realized something funny: I only know their first names—the family above—and I've only had conversations with them separately... long conversations, actually—and tours... They say that they're related...and they do look alike... *Mamma Maria* (she

---

[64] *Macelleria*. Butcher shop

works the terraces all day); Pop-Pop (runs the fish store with his buddies); Domenico (son #1, and all that comes with that, inclusive of the pretty wife); Giulio (son #2 who is flawlessly remodeling an old cantina [apparently a popular thing in these parts] adjacent to our place in the authentic and artistic of manner—conserving the old olive press and making it part of his new six-room B&B's bar); and Luca (son #3, and all that comes with that, he works the land with Maria). Luca and our Alberto are buddies, apparently, and Alberto tells me that Luca loves to come up to his place, in Agerola. Their garden is about the same size as this garden (four terraces approximately 125-150 yards long) minus the villa. It is all grapes, vegetables, weeds, peas, artichokes, more weeds, flowers, figs, oranges and assorted blossoming trees. These are real working class/middle class Italians. They put in a long day. Oh, and last month, their new fancy wall at the B&B project completely caved in on the garden directly below and next to ours, so they are going to be bringing a bunch of mules through my new vegetable garden next week to begin the repairs. Lovely. They first have to remove the tons and tons of rocks and rubble and then begin the rebuilding process (which is slated to take two months) because the crew only works after their regular jobs. (Who knew asses were in such high demand, but they are.) And to access this property from the road above, the ass-man and his crew, constructed ramps with scaffolding, poles and timber to breach terrace upon terrace (this is for mules with heavy loads) until ultimately reaching our place and then, from there, they will have to cross my vegetable garden to the neighboring garden. It is even longer and more difficult than it sounds. Crazy. But, what is one to do except accommodate? Especially when I've been asked to do so. Thank God nobody was under the wall when it went. Walls are a big deal these days in Montebello. It seems that someone's wall fell on someone else's head last year somewhere here in Italy and the wall's owner was held liable and was sent to prison. Now everyone is paranoid about their ageing walls and the town is backlogged with repair requests— hence the busy mules. And to make matters even more complicated, if one lives on a *via*[65] with recently remodeled stairs (as we do), then no

---

[65] *Via*. Passageway, walkway

mules are allowed on those stairs—meaning you have to negotiate with your neighbors to ingress / egress their gardens with your mule train. Totally normal. (This is why I love it here so much.)

Chicken has been on for 30 minutes and is beginning to brown ☺... I'll add carrots in 30 minutes... time to build a fire... laundry is on the line... I guess it will be all the fresher when it dries tomorrow (it is raining)...

Starting fires isn't such a daunting task, as it was when Vicki and I were figuring out the learning curve. I do feel somewhat inadequate for using the fire starters though—but I'm getting over it. (The lingering smell of creosote on one's fingers is somewhat disconcerting though.)

Candles are the next layer of mood...and Angela finally received cream-colored candles as opposed to the white. I find a cream-colored candle illuminates such a nicer color than the white... Angela and her husband, Salvatore, run the *alimentari*[66] where we (I) do most my shopping. Bello, on the other hand, shops the entire village ☺ I shop Angela because they deliver. And when I do venture out, it is always with the dogs and we live hundreds of steps up from Angela's. Jackie needs to be carried up stairs: you do the math. Their son, Luca (there are only about 10 names for guys around here) has a new daughter, runs his own gym during the "off season" for locals, and delivers for his parents... it reminds me of the other night when Salvatore met me at the bottom of our stairs with the forgotten bag of dairy from the day's earlier delivery on his absolutely fabulous vintage Vespa, in his even more fabulous old baby blue, cashmere sweater – total class. Here, taste abounds, even on the most pedestrian of levels. Our groceries were delivered—to the kitchen—while I was in the garden pruning around an old arbor that I, unwittingly, had severed its old-growth jasmine last fall when I was a bit overzealous with my new pruners. (Think 20 years of overgrowth.) It will look stellar in the coming year.

---

[66] *Alimentari.* All-purpose grocer and household goods store

Sometimes you have to make some hard choices around here between immediate aesthetic satisfaction and long-term betterment of the villa. And sometimes, you just make a bad cut.

...The fire is roaring, the carrots are in the oven, and I am chiming out. It's 7 p.m. More with my 7 a.m. espresso... but Luca's red wine is really tasty, fyi. Glad that you are here with me, right now. At least in my thoughts. JJ

Chicken is almost finished... ☺

...Up at 6.45 for the pooches and they are both cuddled together in Jackie's bed—predictable. Here, a foregone conclusion isn't such a bad thing when it is something that you are enjoying. At home, I loathe the thought, but here it means that everything is *tutto posto*[67] (as it should be). Jackie seems to be doing much better with the stairs and negotiating the right ways to travel the grounds. I don't have to follow her about as I did in the early weeks here. Yesterday, she and Rocket had haircuts. Rocket had a full-on Mohawk going on and it was getting gross. Jackie tolerated a bit of a cut because she knew treats were in store...she then had a lovely hot bath and actually danced around the entire villa afterwards. Dancing, spinning around, running about—apparently she really needed a bathing...the family up above also has a dog named Gregorio (Greg for locals) who is an Irish something or other and isn't the brightest bulb in the shop but has a heart of gold. His family lets him run amok and then yells at him and he responds... but when Gregorio comes to visit us there are rules. Of course there are. There is no "unnecessary" barking—leaving room for their own interpretation—because dogs do speak to one another here with much more acceptance than in the States. Sometimes Jackie goes to upper *orto* (vegetable garden) and simply barks to other dogs...they all do it. Rocket isn't a barker though—unless it is regarding a cat or stranger on the grounds, then he goes ballistic.

And my Bello...you may ask...he's on a plane right now returning from the States. He had an appointment in Oklahoma City this week. He was

---

[67] *Tutto posto.* In its place

gone for four days. That would be like coming to Italy for *pranzo*[68] and then returning to California the next day. He is going to be home for the next 10 days! After a week or so, he likes to bust out of here… this place is remote if you haven't gotten the gist.

Today I am going to deal with the laundry above (I am hoping that it will be a hot day) and wash the bedding and hang that to dry… First, I need to install another clothesline—the existing is already full. After that, I will most likely do some quick gardening (I like all the paths perfect at least every other day), pick some oranges for friends (already pressed and consumed a pint before espresso), and shave before Bello comes home. I look like Grizzly Adams—sort of. I do have the carcass from last night's chicken (minus the breasts—Bello only eats white meat) that I will turn into a lovely chicken stock (can't buy it in stores here) and put in the freezer for future risotto. I'll start that slow-cooking process in a moment—after my second coffee (it takes both working burners on the stove to warm the milk and espresso). My kitchen is its own dedicated note for one to really get the picture ☺

And the garden: well, the wisteria is as if on steroids and the roses are beginning to pop. I've liberated all of the citrus trees on the lower two terraces and the grumpy old uncle hasn't caught me in the act personally, but I have been spotted by neighbors—most of whom are delighted to see this feral part of the garden (that is fully visible from the village) cleaned up after so many years. There is the awful and thorny bush that spreads like wildfire and covers everything—even fruit trees and eventually kills the tree unless removed. And to remove this plant you have to first cut away at the entire bush, remove that, let it dry for a few days and then go for the root system. If you don't remove the roots, then the plant is back in two weeks—rain or not. It is simply awful. Oh, and if you scratch yourself on the plant, be prepared to wake up in the middle of the night itching like a madman for two or three nights… I wear heavy armor-like attire for the task. And I try to blend in with the foliage because grumpy has been merely yards away on his terrace when I've been cleaning and pruning… it is a really odd comedy.

---

[68] *Pranzo*. Lunch

I did discover that the sour orange tree (actually the tree that was decapitated ten years ago during the feud and now it is comprised of five perfect shoots) is in actuality a fabulous tangerine tree. The fruit is enormous and getting very sweet. Fortunately I have the only keys to the gate that accesses this part of the villa... I also discovered a peach tree that is a remnant of the older peach trees from the terrace above. This tree is about six years old and a bunch of flowers, so there should be good peaches in a couple of months... The fig trees have had their bases freed from weeds and morning glory—which is the other great nemesis of the garden and moi.

...It is just now 8 a.m. for me and getting late for you. I hear Jackie's claws clicking about the villa, no doubt looking for me and another treat. Rocket is back in bed—our bed. To be a teenager in Italy...

Baci ed abbracci[69],

James

---

[69] *Baci ed abbrocci.* Kisses and hugs

Year 2 Living Abroad

8. May and June in Italia

So much happens in a week. Right now it 11:45 *in mattina* and Bello is down for an unusual morning nap accompanied by Rockettino and Jackie is *contento* during laps around a stuffed chair in the *salotto*[70] all while shelling freshly picked peas in the kitchen while smelling the two beautiful bowls of mandarin oranges that Angela sent up with Bello this morning, apparently ideal for *marmalata*[71]. The peas were a gift from my new bff (best friends forever for those of you not up on generation Z slang) Leonardo—and his lovely *moglie*[72]. Remember them? Two weeks ago—Giuliana and the flying glass episode in the *giardino*[73]. Well, as I said, I'd bring him some marmalade; I did the other day while he was in the lowest terrace of his garden, which abuts the highest terrace of this *giardino*. We had a nice chat and come to find out it wasn't him in the garden on the other "incident" day. We don't know who it was. Sometimes things are best left where they lie—I mean lay. Whatever. You know what I mean. It gets better—way better. So, yesterday, I am in the roof terrace next to the *colombaia*[74] and I see Luca and Leonardo having a visit over their mutual, sort of, fence. I think to myself how nice it is to see the two actually chatting. (Luca's brother, Domenico, is rebuilding the stone house in the garden above us and his other brother, Giulio, runs/built their very cool new bed and breakfast on their other property, above the sister of Mario, who lives next to us, that had the wall fall down last year and required the mules and all of that...) This is after I find out from Domenico that he had never really spoke with the man and Giulio said the same. After our mutual *"ciao ciao,"* Leonardo gestures for me to come up, come up. He then gets the

---

[70] *Salotto.* Living room
[71] *Marmalata.* Marmalade
[72] *Moglie.* Wife
[73] *Giardino.* Garden
[74] *Colombaia.* Pigeon house, dovecote

translation conformation from Luca (voices travel on the hillside) and yells "come here, come here." I think he expected me to climb the wall, again. That was out of the question. I don't make a practice of scaling the walls around here. That would be perceived as odd. Walls are sacred zones that people are not supposed to cross—regardless of height— at any time, other then in the most extreme of situations, as demonstrated the other week. Rocket and I decided to accept his invitation and out the gate we headed and up the stairs to find out exactly where Leonardo lived.

Back to Leonardo

Things are so often not what we expect and we so often get what we want when it is unexpected. Ironic it is. In my case I wasn't expecting such a warm and authentically enthusiastic greeting by both Leonardo and his wife (who immediately scurried into the dark entrance of the pristine white villa to retrieve something sure to be terrific) as I was beeped in their gate, and, I've always wanted to see this particular garden from above as it has the coolest, undulating circular stepping-stone pattern that from above is very arty. I thought someone else lived there and Leonardo in the villa above. Wrong. That belongs to his cousin who lives on the island of Ischia. Leonardo does have the coolest deposito[75] (a deposito should be very cool indeed—it is where you store your vino[76] and beer) and his is below the house of his cousin—right above our garden... Leonardo's villa is over a bit. Now, as I only saw the outside and the garden (which is appropriate on a first visit), I can say they are very clean and civilized and fully dressed. We sipped homemade fragola[77] liquor and chatted about mutual friends (life-long for him, relatively new ones to me) and such. It was straight out of a Twilight Zone episode. I was waiting for something outrageously strano[78] to happen, and Rocket knew it because he was sitting on my feet, but the

[75] *Deposito.* Cellar, pantry. A cool, dark, and mostly windowless room, generally under the house for wine production, meat storage, and canned and dried goods – *troppo* important.
[76] *Vino.* Wine
[77] *Fragola.* Strawberry
[78] *Strano.* Strange

feeling passed and we kept it light and easy and skirted the whole "recycling" incident. So, shelling these peas made me think about jotting this down and filling you in. Never a dull moment in neighbor maintenance.

Versailles in Napoli

Another tale. This was the day before yesterday. Bello has always wanted to see the Italian version of Versailles named Reggia di Caserta[79] *and we chose Saturday to be that day. So we rented a car and packed up the dogs and off we went. We wanted to go with Claudia but she wasn't able to come. So, we are arriving to the castle, palazzo— Villa...whichever—it's big, huge, and then we are suddenly diverted another route by some man in blue jeans and a white tee-shirt (as in an undershirt) and I thought that was certainly a bit odd as was his somewhat elevated excitement level, but I let it slide—but it definitely registered as strano... who in god's name would let this person come to work dressed so inappropriately... "Casual Friday" doesn't exist here... nice jeans... but why the undershirt...? he was weird... there was something about that guy... all at the same time. We proceeded down the street to be further directed into an abandoned lot, complete with pre-war buildings and overgrown trees, where a third, casually (poorly) dressed person is shouting out orders to us—and this is Naples and to be considered shouting one has to be pretty darn excited about something—more exciting then parking—that I was certain of. I was also certain that we were leaving the situation—subito. I don't even know if those cars were there at the end of the day. I can say for certain that the characters were not. And there was plenty of nice, cool, underground parking at the castle.*

---

[79] *Reggia di Caserta.* The Royal Palace at Caserta – just inland from Naples – is a former royal residence, was constructed by the House of Bourbon-Two Sicilies as their main residence during the 18th century. Upon entering – although smaller and clearly for anything match the grandeur—one nevertheless feels as if they have been transported to Versailles.

I would be hard pressed to make this kind of stuff up.

Angela sent up some beautiful mandarin oranges. I think I will make a nice marmalade with them today and some fresh pasta to go with these peas. I'll do the peas with prosciutto and pasta *scialatielli*[80].

Bello and the dogs are all up.

The Art of the Nap

... It is already the middle of May. Time flies this time of year here. The sun is now setting several minutes a day later and also rising earlier *in mattina* it seems. Factor in the longer day, with the increased heat in *pomeriggio* (the afternoon), and you get the perfect excuse for taking a nap—as opposed to the winter months where one naps because there is simply nothing else to do and your bed tends to be the warmest place in the house. Italy, in general, seems to have two speeds: dormant and full throttle. We are definitely in the latter of the two now.

Marmalata and the Grumpy Zio

Updates: This being the year of marmalade, I guess we will start there. Two days ago I jarred what I think will be the last of the citrus marmalade for the year. Three months of lemons and oranges have my cupboard full (after countless gifts to neighbors, friends, and service providers) and my interest is waning—although marmalade is a much more complex and interesting culinary product to produce than it is readily given credit for. You realize this after you prepare no fewer than 15 batches in the course of one season. So much depends on the quality of the fruit and its skin. This is determined by the rainfall from the preceding months and the surroundings of the tree from the year before, for weeds and vines covering your citrus will not allow proper sunlight or water to reach the leaves and roots, respectively. Then, there is the quality of the soil and the actual shape of the tree and whether or not it has been maintained and pruned and most

---

[80] *Scialatielli*. A thick and short fettuccine-like pasta. Originating on the Amalfi Coast, it is a local specialty and a staple of Campania cuisine.

importantly, whether the tree feels like you care about it or not. Well, this year, the trees down in my contested secret garden were stupendous—outrageous, actually. If you recall, for the past two years, I have been laboring down below, first uncovering the trees from years of weeds and roses and morning glory assaults, which had the lower trees teetering on utter destruction from their own weight and parasites. Well, this year there was so much fruit on the trees that they were breaking branches from the weight of their own production. You can't have fruit-bearing trees survive on their own without proper care or they simply implode on themselves from the neglect, and there is very little more a travesty then seeing a 20- or 30- or 40-year-old fruit tree seeing its demise simply from lack of care or attention—tragic it is. Of course all of this seems a little too sweet and simple and all for reality, and you are right, for what is beauty without its contrast? Grumpy *Zio*[81] offered up all the contrast needed, of course. If you recall, the lower two tiers are the shared tiers with *zio*, a few *zias*[82] and several cousins (of whom I have only seen and have yet to meet, formally)—none of whom pay any attention to the space other than staring at it from across the street. It was the other day, when Alberto was here with the weed killer to do battle with the *erbacce*[83] down below at the request of Lady Marchese (I think the thought of my weeding in the public's eye makes her a bit nervous, she being a lady and all, and my being of guest of hers), so I thought it best to let grumpy *Zio* know what we we're up to because he was on his usual stoop and watching our every move. It didn't go well. I wasn't surprised after the fact, but every time I engage the old fart I can't help but hope that this time, this one time, the outcome from our interaction might be fruitful (pun intended)—and this time was no exception to my past disappointments. I offered him lemons (there were no more oranges to offer for those made the most exceptional marmalade weeks ago), but he, of course, rudely declined and told me that he knew I had been taking the fruit—which let me to a polite but stern retort explaining that I too was well aware that I had

---

[81] *Zio*. Uncle
[82] *Zias*. Italianglish for "aunts"
[83] *Erbacce*. Weeds

been picking the fruit—for how else would they have been picked. I hate it when people tell me the obvious. I'm not stupid. Full tree versus empty tree... one doesn't have to attend *università* (that is how they refer to college here) to figure that out. I explained (or tried to) that it was necessary for the trees to have their fruit picked when they are flowing (or the next year's crop will suffer). He didn't seem to care and just barked at me in the local dialect. *Tu non e* blah, blah, blah, blah, blah. I simply asked him a second time if he would like me to bring him a bag and after his subsequent secondary barking I bid him goodbye—in English. We then went about our business. I may just bring him some marmalade. Oh, here's the good part... so the next morning, I am going down to the street for some reason or another (don't recall the exact reason), and I notice a bright and shiny new lock and even shinier new chain on the first garden gate that enters the lower terrace—a lock and chain. Well, you know who did it—*Zio*. Come to find out, he had been sneaking over the past two nights and simply wiping out any citrus that he could reach. Ok, so it's his fruit too, I realize that, and it's not my property (I *kind of* realize that as well), but I spent two months clearing the bloody path just so one could access the garden, so I do have a certain sense of entitlement regarding the space. Of course having Lady Marchese's backing certainly adds credibility and credence to the situation as well. Here's the fun part... so grumpy knows that I know that he knows that I know that he locked the gate below (I enter the lower garden from our garden above) and he camps out for the entire day in his roof-top loggia room just watching the lower terrace to see if he can catch me picking the last of the lemons. I waited until he fell asleep while reading his book and I immediately went down and pruned the lemon tree in question (it had been at least 15 years since its last pruning at it showed) and then I picked some of the really high lemons, as the ladder was handy. Well, this last batch of lemon marmalade rivals the best of the season. This batch, I soaked the lemons in fresh water for 50 hours before cooking and the results were, again, as different and unique as all the other batches. Perhaps working in the absence of a recipe yields these results.

Enough of grumpy *Zio*—at least for now, the fig tree has another good week of ripening so we have a bit of a respite from the entire scene.

Gelso (Mulberry Jam)

Yesterday was the first day of making gelso (mulberry) jam—and it is a messy and time-consuming process. I haven't tasted the first batch yet— chilling a bottle in the fridge now... I will bring up a bottle to the due donne[84] *staying in the* colombaia *this month. It is the mother (and her friend) of the new guy that rented the* colombaia *for the year. I have yet to meet him—no one has, except Generoso—not even Vivianna. Well, the ladies have settled in and are getting the rhythm of the villa. We've had a few moments where we have gotten to understand each other and my issues of privacy and wanting to simply be left alone. We're getting there. Rocket likes visiting the ladies and Mama is warming up to him. Her friend really likes him. They're a cute couple. I was wishing for a* nonna[85] *around here to help me out—I might have gotten what I wished for, but double. That wouldn't surprise me. One has to be careful what one wishes for because the universe does provide. What we do with what is presented to us is solely based on the individual though. More to follow... but I think I will ask the ladies to watch over the other ladies (our chickens) while we are away at the end of the month—we are going to the South—the Deep South. Giuliana and Stefano have a place in Lecce. Actually, two places down there. One is in Lecce and the other along the seashore. We are staying at the seashore place for it has a walled in garden for the dogs and me. I'll bring my gloves and sheers for certain. Give me a somewhat abandoned garden space and, well, you know where that leads—nirvana. I am glad that were going on a road trip—it should be a riot. Giuliana told us that we could also bring the chickens and that she had a chicken coop. Of course she does and of course we could—it is the south of Italy and it wouldn't seem that out of place—our stopping at an* Autogrill[86] *for a coffee with our rambunctious*

---

[84] *Due donne.* Two women
[85] *Nonna.* Grandmother
[86] *Autogrill.* An ever-present feature on the Italian *autostrade*, Autogrill is a highway rest stop-cum-fast food establishment known for everything from

teen-aged terrier growling out the window, Jackie Chan passed out in the back seat, and four chickens in a crate in the back. But I think the chickens would find the whole excursion a bit stressful in fact. It was very sweet of Julie and Stefano to make accommodations for us all though. I can't wait to see the Deep South again. Lecce will be the furthest we have gone down the "boot" of Italia. There should be some interesting stories to come...

Gian Sopra, Gian Sotto, and Dining with Bachelors

So, Gianluca (referred to as *Gian sopra* which means "Gian above" last year as opposed to Gianpaolo who was referred to as *Gian sotto* which means "Gian below" last year) did not return this year to the *colombaia*, thus the new nonnas—just an FYI. But Gianpaolo is back this year much more than last. He has the *casa* below next to the Ballarati's and Alessandro and his girlfriend, Alessandra, stayed there almost all spring and summer last year. It seems that one either works all the time around here or not at all. There seems to be no "in between" anything around here. Hot or cold, sunny or rainy, nice or rude—everything is one or the other. More to follow with JP (*Gian sotto*) for I think he will be a bit more of a fixture this year. (He's around late thirties and practices law in Milano and his mother knows Lady Marchese and they have been friends forever. You have to know someone to get a foot in the door around here and once one's foot is in, there is little reason to want to pull it out—unless it is kicked out, that is. And the latter rarely happens.)

An Italian Bachelor's[87] Dinner Party

... Dinner at JP's was epic. Bachelors throw the funniest dinner parties. And most often that is because I don't think the host considers that guests would stay past cocktails. So, in our case, it was an impromptu

---

espresso to *panini* and to *panettone* as a gift stop during the holidays. Think Howard Johnsons of the 1960s and 70s US interstate system.

[87] "Bachelor." Generally not to be confused unnecessarily with independence. A "bachelor" in Italy will always have a room at mother's. And, most likely, an Italian bachelor will not have truly mastered any skills of domesticity.

pasta dinner (what else) prepared by Stefano. I contributed a few items like parmesan and oregano (Stefano asked for *prezzemolo*, which is parsley, and I figured the two sound alike... the substitution did not go unnoticed—even after the chef's two gin and tonics.) Back to the table... present was Rocket and myself and Stefano, as well as Christiana who has a great home up the hillside here in Montebello where Generoso brought Bello and me to for a dinner party two years ago—she lives in Paris. She had a girlfriend, Mary, along and there was a very sweet girl from Bologna, named Claudia, who was staying in Positano. The girls were all the invited quests of playboy Tomaso who was staying the night at JP's from where he was departing for Capri the following day because he was sponsoring a boat for the Capri regatta to advertise his new art website—whatever that means. He told me "people with boats should know about my site," all right, as they should. After pasta was served and eaten, it seemed that dinner was over (one course is just fine with me) so I thought it would be fun to take the guests for a garden walk— Italians without gardens make for the absolute best tour guests because everything nature oriented is so bloody foreign to them that it is a kick to share in—and the fireflies were in full force so it seemed the appropriate thing to do. Well, Mary from Paris freaks out at the fireflies and thinks that they are some lighting strand that I've rigged up to scare her, Tomaso and Christiana never make it past the grand terrace, and Stefano and Claudia are deep in conversation at the by-now wax-covered table (it was breezy and we were dining outdoors by candles) and JP is "asleep" on the outside *divano*[88] and there is a big piece of sausage on the table—untouched. Hilarious. Rocket and I went home. He threw up. This is why we dine at home. And, why we don't drink gin and tonics.

That was a few days back... Bello was in Milan that night—no, he had just returned from Milan and he was off to America that night— Saturday night, to be exact. (All the days and weeks and months seem to roll right into one another and because it is here and foreign and isolated and all, and there aren't the same points of daily reference that

---

[88] *Divano*. Couch

punctuate life at home so it is easy to lose track of exactly when something occurred—hence the journal.) Back to Bello: he's been at home for most of the past month—with the exception of the two-day Milan trip (which was a senior European corporate management strategic meeting that Bello was invited to attend) and another two-day trip to Frankfurt (more collaborating with the Europe offices). He has been asked by the London office to please come up for a visit as well. They all love him here. No surprise. Right now he is in Mississippi assisting that office with a proposal. Never a dull moment in my Bello's world. He's been off the running for two weeks now, ever since he and some upstart Italian runner that he knows decided to run with one another and, apparently push one another, and Bello returned home walking and with a pulled hamstring. He will be in the sea before we know it though. Time for a second coffee...

Today is Wednesday the 20th—A mere month from the longest day of the year and the eve of my little sister's birthday—one of my favorite days of the year, actually. And the next 30 days, or so, leading up to the solstice are the best for being here on the Costierra.

Claudia, Gelato, and a Posi Visit

... So, last week, Claudia and I are out on a little *giro* because I hadn't seen her in more then a month (she's currently undergoing chemo for breast cancer, hence my shaved head, and we don't get to spend as much time together as I would like) and we decide to go to Positano for a gelato. Along the way we stopped at Posiflora so I could pick certain colored geranium for delivery. You see, the preceding week, Bello phone-ordered for me (in Italian) deep purple geraniums to be delivered (20 of them) but what arrived were fuchsia geraniums. I really am not fond of fuchsia and as the exact same thing happened last year when I phoned in a geranium order I thought Bello's efforts would lessen (or eliminate) the chances of a repeat—I was wrong. So with the 20 fuchsia from the preceding week painstakingly placed and planted (I don't do returns—particularly with plants—for that is how one gets a bad reputation amongst service providers), I was determined to get the colors that I wanted. But that would be far too predictable. So Claudia and I show Marco the two colors that I am solely interested in: dark (*scuro*) purple and *scuro rosso* (red)—pretty simple, I though. Needless to say what arrived two days ago wasn't exactly what I wanted, or ordered, but such is life. The 20 deep purple geranium (an odd color and not always easy to find as they had to be collected from the green house, thus the three-day lag time) were present but, somehow, my 20 *scuro rosso* became 20 two-tone fuchsia. Poor Dario (he delivered last week's mistake as well). I told him they were perfect and tipped him handsomely. I figured that I obviously didn't communicate clearly enough and now my task was to find a place for more yet more fuchsia in the garden. Fortunately (I say that now), we have some fuchsia existing already in the garden in the form of heirloom geraniums (fuchsia, pink and burnt orange are typical Amalfi Coast summer-colored geraniums and the deeper colored geraniums are more recently propagated varieties and subsequently not quite as durable during the harsh winter months) as well as some fuchsia roses—both I have never been so thrilled about. Well, after combining the two fuchsia colored geraniums (one solid and the other two-tone with white) and placing them in mass around the other fuchsia plantings, the result is actually quite something—if you like fuchsia that is. I'll probably be ripping them all out next year.

It is now the end of May and it feels as if we are definitely entering the summer months. Jackie Chan likes to sleep most of the day and we have to wake her every so many hours or she stays up all night pacing about like a teenager after a double espresso. Last night we were up at 1, 2, 3, and 4 in the morning. Such is life. I finally convinced her to go to bed after she fell asleep on the floor in the kitchen in front of her food bowl. She does love breakfast time. She only walks in counter-clockwise circles now, so you have to watch her when she gets near corners of the house with furnishings for she gets trapped under chair legs and tables and just about anything larger then she is. Rocket sleeps through all the commotion though—like a teenager. So does my bello (although I think he feigns sleep, sometimes).

A Moment in Time

May becomes June in Italia. This afternoon's (6:00 p.m.) scene (and I am not making this up): it is pouring rain, Rocket is resting in the 1950's contemporary, low-to-the-ground armchair, Jackie Chan is sleeping off her holiday on pillows on the rug, Bello is in town at the market for a nothing in particular, but something necessary, nonetheless... (I mentioned it's raining)... homemade pasta drying in the kitchen and fresh zucchini (from our garden, already) and spring onions—both sliced and ready to be sautéed later, a couple of eggs for the pasta dish (thickens the sauce) from our chickens, and me sitting with some tea and leftover pistachios from Apuglia, while wearing a black-white-and-green clay mask on my face—that is the third part (and marks the end) of my three-hour (post-shaving) rainy-day facial experience—so it seemed the perfect time to write to you.

Off to See Stefano and Guiliana in Apulia[89]

What a difference this week has made. I know if mentioned a million times how quickly things change around here (besides the downpour we are in the middle of right now) and how fast my tomatoes grow and on and on as I can and do often—but this is about Jackie. This past weekend we had all been in Lecce visiting Giuliana and Stefano. They have a beyond fabulous place in the center of the historic district overlooking one of the most beautiful Baroque churches in the entire city as well as a really cool, circa early 1960s house at the beach in San Caltado (10 kilometers/6 miles east of Lecce) which is where Bello and the dogs and I stayed. I was in seventh heaven because we had room for the dogs to roam and Bello had a nice desk to work from with internet and phone available so he could keep up on work and I had the pleasure

---

[89] *Apulia.* A most-special region in southeastern Italy, also referred to as "Puglia." For map-lovers, it is the heel of the boot, extending deep into the Mediterranean and separating the Adriatic Sea from the Ionian. Near Eastern influences are present throughout the region given their shared history of trade and relative proximity. The region is flush with agriculture (think olives and grain) and its cities are rich with culture and unique architecture (from the conical homes of the trulli in Alberobello to the baroque cathedrals of Lecce).

of being given *carte blanche* to organize and tidy and rearrange and feng shui the entire beach house to my heart's content. It was fun. This isn't any ordinary beach house, by the way. Giuliana's father is an architect (as is Giuliana) and this is the house he designed during the 1960s. It is totally cool. It has five, smartly designed and interactive levels that comprise a dozen or more rooms that create two completely different living spaces under one roof. Think of the Brady's house of "The Brady Bunch" and put it on steroids and keep all the props and accoutrement period-perfect and throw in a circa 1980s *Architectural Digest* cover-worthy great room/entry and place it in the southeastern-most corner of Italy (where you can see across the Adriatic to the coast of Albania on a clear day), surround it with a huge wall topped with fascist-era metal spikes (overgrown with colorful roses, or course) and you get the picture. It was familiar feeling, yet oh so foreign. But Jackie loved it. She had a foyer that measured 30x30 feet and absolutely devoid of furnishings (both our kind of foyer), so she could do her circles in peace and did so for endless hours all three days. On our last night, we went into town and brought the dogs. I tried to give Jackie the chance to come along but she wasn't up to the challenge, although a big part of her still really wanted to go. The great part is that in the process of determining if she was up for the challenge of walking a city block, while under the guidance of a leash, Jackie walked a straight line for the first time in months. And the really great part is that she did so again while walking her "via" out our front door. It is like she needed to reboot her directional compass and the walk on the leash did just that. Though right now she is walking circles in this room's foyer—she's up from her nap, Bello is back from the store (apparently we needed milk) and the rain has stopped. Rockettino just popped his head up and is contemplating investigating a barking friend outdoors, but has made the sensible choice. And my tomatoes must have grown at least one foot while we were away. It is time for some Italian news perhaps (always amusing and good practice)—and a fire in the fireplace.

Gagliano Realization

And another clarification from past news: There are four Gagliano brothers, not three as I previously have stated. I had met the other brother, Nicola, the eldest, before—but I did not realize that he was a brother and I hadn't mentioned his name before. Nicola lives in Milano with his long-time partner and he also has a place here in Montebello— way up at the top of the village. I may mention them again—very nice guys. I had been invited up to pick some beans last night. Luca planted their entire four terraces (5 yards by 100 yards long) of grapes with an understory of various vegetables and now he and his mother have about an acre of produce that needs to be weeded and tended to and picked and watered and on and on... Caterina Ballarati once said to me: "James, the orto[90] makes the man morto[91]." Vegetable gardens are rewarding, but a tremendous amount of work. Nonetheless, I think everyone should have the experience.

Saying Goodbye to Your Dog[92]

Saying goodbye to your dog is not something you plan on. You plan on the eventuality of it, but never the day. Today is that day.

I have two of the best dogs anyone could ask for. It just that one of my dogs is dying. I haven't felt this way since I was twelve and I read that wonderful book entitled *Old Yeller*—perhaps you know of it. When the boy's dog dies in the arms of his master I remember crying and thinking to myself why anyone would write such a fantastic story of adventure, trials and triumphs only to have the fabled yellow Lab die in the end. That's just the way it is. Try telling that to a twelve-year-old without breaking their spirit. I was so upset that I just closed the book, never to open it again. Perhaps I will get a copy and read it to the end this time, for I am pretty much passed the shock that was before me then.

We took Jackie Chan off of her regular sedation while we were in Lecce last week and, ever since then, she seems to be enjoying her cognitive

---

[90] *Orto.* Vegetable garden
[91] *Morto.* Dead
[92] You *will* cry.

senses returning and walking in straight lines, as opposed to her tight circles of late. Yesterday morning was typical of most—she woke, peed, went back to bed and woke again around nine for a morning walkabout. (Right now she is trying to make herself comfortable but to no avail... she's down... she fading... thank god... she is resting... she's snoring.) But this morning was a bit different—she somehow jumped the wall that has kept her safe all this time and ended up in the yard down below of Maestro Domenico. Nothing broke this time, with the exception of her spirit—from 10 feet above I could see it in her body language that she was visibly confused and she was frightened because she couldn't see where she was. She is ready for this to stop. She knows it. She keeps walking towards the light in the house. She will not eat (not even prosciutto or a fresh egg) and she isn't interested in drinking water this morning for the first time ever. I've already called our veterinary doctor, Antonio, and he will be here this afternoon and we will put her down to rest. She will be more comfortable.

Jackie has had one hell of a fun week. Last week at this time we were in Lecce and she was having the time of her life—she roamed the house and garden and thoroughly enjoyed the open spaces of Giuliana and Stefano's beach house—walking about independently and having a genuinely good time and smiling all the day. She tried new food and smelled lots of new smells. Since returning to Montebello, she has been a very busy girl, attending a dinner party last night and spending quality time with Bello (who left for America this morning). (I've insisted that he take breaks from his work and walk her several times a day because I felt that he may not have the opportunity when he returned—I hate being right this time— and I am so glad that he did.)

An Animal's Lasts...

Four hours later... You never think of a person's or animal's "lasts" until it is happening. In our case it is *last* drink, *last* walk in the garden, *last* time being able to walk in a circle on her own. That's where we are at present. I just freshened her bedroom bed for what I am sure will be the *last* time, and I am proud to say that I never regretted having to do it a single time. My *principessa*[93] is having a peaceful last day. And my *principe*[94] is being a trooper and staying close at hand and paying extra special attention to his queen. I am desperately trying to stay very busy and get things *tutto posto* so I can check out later. I have to dig her grave too—some things are best done alone, and with your dog.

His Final Farewell

Done. But in our case we had Claudia to help—thankfully. And as a justified poetic ending to a brief love affair, Rocket disappeared for a few minutes after all of today's goings-on—and returned without his Cowboy Up![95] *bandana—a first, well, actually, a second—nevertheless, sans signature scarf. I continued watering the main walk and when I made it closer to Jackie's new spot in the garden I flashed on the cowboy of the Wild West leaving his cherished bandana on the grave of the love of his life that was taken from him too soon... I rounded the corner and there was his scarf in the hole he had made in the center of her grave. I left it there. And he now wears her leather collar.*

****

And that was then. Yesterday was a pretty rotten day. I managed to call my mother and give her the heads up. Called Alison and Billi and Jeffrey and Hannah, too. Jackie was quite popular. I phoned our friend and pet physic, Patrice Ryan, as well. She already knew, of course. Not that she knew specifically but she flashed on us yesterday while she was driving in Los Angeles. It seems that Jackie was getting the word out.

A Really Private Moment

I held her while she was given the injection. By that time though, she was comfortably resting because about a half an hour before the vet arrived, she woke, wanted to go out and pee, walk a few steps and eat a

---

[93] *Principessa*. Princess
[94] *Principe*. Prince
[95] Bello brought back a collection of bandanas from a long-established Western / ranch wear outpost during his last trip to Denver. Rocket's favorite was the dark blue bandana with the horseshoes and "Cowboy Up!" print.

little something. I know these things by now—so we did just that. I had prepped her breakfast with all her remaining travel sedatives in hopes of her resting through the day as we waited for Antonio (both the longest and the shortest days of mine in recent memory), but she wouldn't eat or drink all the day until that last little meal—eggs and prosciutto—her favorite things and her favorite thing to do. We dined and that was when I said goodbye and reminded her for a countless time how special of a dog and what a good friend she was to Bello and me and to Rockettino as well. She grunted and went to sleep. She sleeps best on a full stomach. *Dorme bene*[96] Jackie Chan...

We went for a walk this morning with JP (Gian-sotto[97]) to San Domenico Convent and brought the Gagliano dog Gregorio along—he's just learning what a leash is—it was interesting. And the Family Marchese just left this afternoon after an unexpected, but very pleasant visit and we are now getting ready to go to Positano with Claudia for the evening—a busy day, indeed.

A Dog's Year

Something to think about: if dog years are calculated roughly as seven per one human year, then one could calculate a dog's day as one of our weeks. Therefore, even an hour of a dog's life is significant. Remember that next time you have the opportunity to give a nice dog a pat on the head and a kind smile. I think that is why they say that dogs never forget—they simply move on—because I believe that they know how precious their time here really is.

Thank you for a wonderful ten years Jackie Chan—I will always remember you.

Hypocrisy – it is what it is...

Alas, it is finally June.

---

[96] *Dorme bene.* Sleep well
[97] Gian-below

The past few days have been a myriad of emotions and feelings with thoughts of sorrow and recollection, reflections on past experiences and thoughts toward the future sans Jackie Chan. Quite frankly, I am glad to have been alone with Rocket and I truly believe that it has been better for Bello to had been out the door when all this was taking place. He has now had time to process it all and, besides, he couldn't be breaking down in front of colleagues like I could in front of my fruit trees. Regardless of how equal the sexes have become, there is still something disconcerting that our society finds in seeing a grown man cry. Interesting, it is, hypocrisy.

June in Italia Continues...

Time for a second coffee—Tino is passed out from yesterday's unplanned, excursion to Montepertuso[98] with Gregorio. Our plan was to take a hike up to the upper trail, to *an abondonata casa sopra in le mountains*[99]—that was our plan. Gregorio had plans of his own, however, and they included taking a hard left at the fork in the trail and had very little to do with my vision of an afternoon picking wild cherries off the ancient tree at the old *casa*. By the time Rocket and I reached the fork in the trail he was nowhere in sight, which then began the three-hour hunt for the not-so-smart (but very sweet) Irish setter.

The Gagliano Dog Named "Gregorio"

(Remember, Gregorio is part of the Gagliano family who live above us, and they [Luca] found Grego a couple of years ago in the streets of Rome, or was it Naples?—somewhere other than here—and the poor boy has had to learn a lot in a relatively short period of time about how to be somewhat civilized, which, compared to American dog standards, leaves much to be desired. Much.)

---

[98] *Montepertuso*. Small village on the hillside above Positano – another stop on the Path of the Gods. Meaning "hole in the mountain" or "pierced mountain," it is known for its multiple myths that each resulted in a hole in the mountain with its arch visible from multiple vistas along the coast.

[99] Italianglish for "an abandoned summer house up in the mountains."

Fortunately for Rocket and me, the trail was sprinkled with tourists (the lower trail tends to get that way this time of year), so I was able to speak English to them all. Before long, there was a network of Germans and Dutch and English all keeping an eye out for a big red dog. So back and forth Rocket and I go (Rocket in my arms most of the time for the trail gets very steep and rocky on the lower loop), trying desperately to figure out exactly which direction Grego may have gone and pondering just how I would go about explaining how I lost Gregorio to the Gaglianos. After our third run back and forth along the lower to the upper trail section (about two kilometers each way—it is now past noon and getting hotter by the minute), we receive a call from the pack of girls from Holland who had found Gregorio. He wanted to accompany them all the way to Positano. They waited for us while we did the traversing of the trail for a fourth time to retrieve Grego. Needless to say, Rocket and I were exhausted. Gregorio too, he wanted to sit and rest every shady chance that he got while on the way back. I was just glad to have both dogs in my possession, alive. I kept Gregorio on Tino's leash until we reached the village. Gregorio walked himself home. I still want to go pick some cherries off my special tree. And we haven't quite given up on Gregorio, so he can come, too—on another day though.

✼✼✼✼✼✼✼✼✼✼✼✼✼✼✼✼✼

Today we are staying in and I am cooking. *Gelso* berries are already on the stove and I have a big tub of basil to make pesto and some lovely zucchini from the garden that I am going to make Bello a nice zucchini parmesan from (the recipe was given to me last night from Irma's mother [remember the tiff last year?] and her aunt [she was there too])—nothing like a recipe exchange to mend old wounds...

Girls Being Girls

And here is funny tale... since our return from our family visit to Lecce last week our chickens have seemingly been on holiday from laying their eggs, with the exception of Pamela, that is. Four chickens yielding one egg daily.... Not very good math, I figured. I also figured that the cause was simply old age. Wrong, again. Life is so often not what we think it is…. In actuality, the girls had been hiding their eggs in a new nest up in the old chicken coop. I discovered Rosa sitting on a pile of five eggs. It was too cute. I don't think that the birds like Rocket having access to their new coop's nest area (although they have a perch which is high above ground) and that could be why they relocated— now I remember… a few days ago Pamela and Rocket had a fist fight in the coop because Rocket got too close to the nest with an egg in it—it was *hell in a chicken coop* for a few moments. The other reason may be because we had Pina (she lives below us and takes care of the cleaning of the other abodes here because, God forbid, someone clean their own house around here) and her two little girls tend to the chickens while we were in Lecce and, perhaps, the girls (the chickens) did not like strangers taking their eggs. Seems logical—girls will be girls. I haven't your run-of-the-mill chickens, as you can surmise. The funny thing is that I had become resolved to one egg a day from our girls and was planning on having someone (perhaps Pina's girls) tend to them during our off months, so they wouldn't wind up on Alberto's dinner table due to their non-performance. If you don't perform around here then don't count on being welcomed too long—on the Costierra, for nobody, or thing, gets a free ride—the folks around here are too pragmatic for that.

Time to phone in an order to Angela's—Bello comes home tomorrow and we are out of everything that doesn't come from our garden. I tend to live like a monk when Bello is away—only eating what is here and presenting itself. Bello insists on some basic staples though—like milk for his coffee and fresh cheese (daily) and some fresh bread.

I am happy with an *International Herald-Tribune* every few days and home delivery (that's how we get our bubbly)—we haven't become complete purists.

… And we are nearing the Summer Solstice, my favorite day of the year. My little sister, Jamie ("Junebug" to Bello), is born on the eve of the solstice—actually, the longest day of the year. Nature knows this date and starts to prepare for the coming winter the very next day. Although the changes are subtle, they are there, and the more that you look for them, the more they become clear and present. Specifics slip my mind at present—for we just woke—but I will have some observations to share later.

The Villa Gang

Last night was the first of the summer dinners with the villa gang. The Fittipaldis are in, the Ballaratis/Florenas are in, and friends from Santa Barbara are visiting the coast, so we are having one of those Italian, late-night dinners on our terrace. Caterina (being Tuscan and generally all-around fabulous) made a lovely mixed seafood and spaghetti dish accompanied by a Greek chopped salad—she is getting the recipe to Bello and I will share it with you if you like. We sat around the table for hours and chatted and everyone was able to catch up with one another from their busy lives.

Today started with a major thunderstorm coming in from the sea. The thing with thunderstorms is that you see them coming well before you even hear their roar—it is that whole light traveling faster then the speed of sound thing playing itself out in full dramatic fashion. You can count the seconds that it takes for the thunder to arrive after seeing the lightning to get a sense for the distance out the storm is and for the power it is to be delivering. In this case, it was rapid, strong and quickly fleeting, but for fifteen minutes, it was as if the great flood were upon us. I had just enough time to wake (5:45) and remove all the patio cushions and rugs just before the deluge began. And just as quickly as it arrived (and dumped two or so inches), it organized itself for a clean departure. I was back in bed by 6:00. We then slept until 9:00.

What We Do for Appearance

Today I think we will make more fichi[100] *jam. Yesterday I made a white and black fig preserve with mulberries and we tried it this morning. Delicious. It has big chunks of fruit and is colored purple from the* gelso *I added. And there is a cool breeze this morning, so working in the garden will be a welcomed pleasure from the oppressive heat that has characterized the past couple of weeks.... Just in from hanging rugs on*

---

[100] *Fichi.* Figs

the roof—Leonardo sent his salutations—remember Leonardo? The Flying Glass episode last month... people appreciate it when you forgive and forget and don't repeat the tale to their neighbors. I think the latter point resonates most strongly with Leonardo. Claudia explained the possible reasoning best for the flying glass: she said that he probably didn't want his children (and signora and grandchildren) to know how much beer he was actually putting away—so he tossed the evidence over the wall and down the hill. She is probably dead-on right. We do so much for the sake of appearances. Perhaps it is human nature.

Napolitani Guys

Pietro, whose family we share our terrace with, is here this weekend with a group of his Napolitano friends... It is fun to see the twenty something's in action: they arrive at some unknown hour of the morning, sleep until mid-day, mysteriously end up at the beach, and return to the villa just in time for cocktail hour only to repeat the entire process a time or two before disappearing back to Naples for their work week. And you never see them eat a thing. Youth.

Missing My Muse

I'm back... it's been almost two weeks since I last wrote to you—sorry. Life is different now and I have to find myself a new muse. It was always so easy to regale my day with Jackie Chan as part of the equation, but we evolve. We have begun the process. Rockettino still reflects on Jackie from time to time—you can most notice it when he returns to the house from a jovial exercise out in the garden and he realizes that she isn't here to greet him... so he sits in one of his "spots," lets out a sigh, and takes a rest. But these instances are becoming further spaced out in time. Bello had an interesting dream the night before last: he dreamt that he awoke at our Santa Barbara house to the sound of Jackie's collar accoutrement clanking about her neck and when he opened his eyes, there she was playing with Rockettino their favorite game of subtle chase, and then Jackie runs to the front door, which opens on its own and just enough to let her pass—when Bello opened the door behind her, she had vanished. He said she was young and firm and in great spirits. She was letting him know that she was still all right. I believe she was preparing to leave this realm and heading off to that vast place where we all eventually go to await our next assignment. I hope I get to know her again. His tale still makes me tear.

✱✱✱✱✱✱✱✱✱✱✱✱✱✱✱✱✱

It being the last day of the month and all, I thought that I better get cracking in offering up some updates—June is typically a very busy time around here, and this year has been no exception.

Church Bells, Wristwatches, and a Multitude of Polizie

I've come to notice that very few people wear watches around here. And as I type, I hear the church bells telling me that it is 8:45... perhaps that is one of the reasons. The funny thing is, though, that it seems that everything is done in unison here and in a timely manner on the Costierra. When it is time to plant your zucchini—everyone plants their zucchini. When it is time to paint your roof stark white again to reflect the summer sun's relentless rays—everyone paints their roof... and when it is time to do your weeding (apparently I didn't get that memo)—everyone does their weeding—that was done on June 1st. And with the deadline for burning one's garden debris July 1st, everyone is burning this week (never after 5 *in mattina*[101] or only after 8 *in sera*[102] though, and never if there are winds) —green weeds and all (which makes for the most obnoxious smoke imaginable). Last night, it was my turn, and my fires are epic for you can see them all the way from Positano. Last night's burn was no exception. The pile started out at about 5 meters (15 feet) and the flames shot up another 5. This morning, when I went up to let the girls out of their coop, the fire was still smoldering. I find it really strange that one of the most beautiful places in all of Europe, arguably the world, still allow its people to burn their garden waste. For it doesn't necessarily stop with garden debris, that's for certain. Mattresses, old furniture, broken new furniture—it all tends to be fair game, with the exception of plastic—that warrants a call to the environmental police—and I didn't just make that up—

---

[101] *In mattina.* In the morning
[102] *In sera.* In the evening

Environmental Police. Actually, here in Italia, believe it or not, there are all kinds of different "police": there is the *guarda di finanza*, that makes sure everyone is ringing up their sales at all *negozi*[103] (shops); there is the local *polizia*[104] for law enforcement; the parking police; the secret police (that everyone knows about); and I am sure another layer or two that I am not fully aware of—fortunately. And nobody wants to have any dealings with the police in this country—zero. It doesn't tend to be a good thing. Everyone is so dramatic in this country as it is—can you imagine factoring in dramatic *carabinieri*[105]? (I never did get that second coffee.)

Italian Rites of Passage

Another observation that I have made is the various rites of passage that everyone seems to partake in here—and they vary dramatically, determined generally by gender and age. Let's start with the youth. At the earliest age, parents keep their kids out until almost midnight for any halfway decent reason, most often a saint's birthday, which tends to always take place on weekends and during the warmer, summer months. However, kids are glued to their parents around here, until they reach a certain age—around 12 or 13—when then, they are glued to one another. But at that age, only boys hang out with boys and the same goes with the girls—and they travel in packs, arm in arm and the boys tend to be pretty boisterous—the girls a bit more demure. Then there is the cell phone—no gender difference here—they all get one. And fashion suddenly becomes paramount, as if some internal clock goes off in the Italian mind that makes selecting the proper belt to go with those jeans all so important. It is like watching a junior catwalk parading to catch the junior high school bus—it's a riot. And timing is very important when it comes to selecting the right accessories here on the coast—such as when to retire the winter coat and pull out the spring windbreaker, when color replaces black as "the new black" and then when white replaces color as "the new black." All determined by

---

[103] *Negozi.* Shops, businesses
[104] *Polizia.* Civilian police force
[105] *Carabinieri.* The military force who carry out domestic policing duties

the date of the calendar—and usually coinciding with the first or middle of any given month. Do you see why a watch is completely useless here? And this "rite of passage" doesn't stop with the onset of puberty—it just gets started, actually. The teens suddenly reach an age where it is permissible to be out in mixed company and to stay out past midnight. Then it is the scooter, the job, and then marriage. Now, once you've made it to this point, the going gets easy, because everything is preordained. You will have a couple of cute kids that you will dress adorably, your mother and father will tend to fuss over your children and cart them all about the village as if they were just born, you will spend Sundays with your entire family and you will refer to your mother as *mamma*—for all time. If you are male, you will plant a garden— regardless of the size of your yard, and you will take great pride in burning your debris. My god, we're becoming Italian. I don't dress Rocket up though, but I have been known to parade him through the village on rare occasions—usually only after Bello has been on travel for several days and I am desperate for a *Herald-Tribune*.

✱✱✱✱✱✱✱✱✱✱✱✱✱✱✱✱✱✱

But, the month is over, so I have burned my garden debris (only to start another pile today that I'll burn this fall when the moratorium is lifted) and all the weeds are gone and zucchini is finally past its prime— everyone is simply sick of zucchini by now and you can't even give it away—and eggplant is taking its place. I would have some lovely tomatoes, but the hens have taken a liking to my *pomodoro*[106] patch and they deseed all the lower clusters—fortunately, I planted a new, grafted tomato that grows about 4 feet high and my chickens are only about a foot tall. Rocket and I tried to dissuade the girls from harvesting our crop, but that quickly turned into a full on brawl in the garden with Rocket and me defending ourselves from the unified front of the hens— a lesson to be learned by all male readers: *Do not mess with a pack of hens!*—there is safety in numbers and you will be humiliated. We are still trying to get back on their good side. And there is nothing worse

---

[106] *Pomodoro*. Tomato

than a group of hens that are displeased with you. For they let you know, and know, and know… they are on a *bread, feed, zucchini, and tomato diet* now.

Well, the battery is dying on my laptop and I am still contemplating that second coffee. Alberto is supposed to arrive today as is Salvatore, the plumber—I'm not holding my breath though. The plumbing problems are never ending here—things leak and they tend to leak behind a tiled wall and you have to treat everything with kid gloves or you're bound to pull a fixture off a wall. I've been running grey water out to the garden or to the bathroom because our kitchen sink has a bad connecting pipe in the wall and if you run too much water (or any) down the drain it tends to come out on the floor—and that is never considered a good thing, particularly for Silvia and her family (Irma's cousin and Maestro Domenico's daughter) who live below us at that end of the villa. It is almost 10… No gardener, no plumber… I may be free for the day to do my own thing…

When in Rome

I just realized that I haven't mentioned my hair—or rather lack thereof. It's rather serious. Our best friend here on the coast is battling breast cancer and I thought hair just wasn't so necessary. When in Rome, right? We find out soon if there will be more treatments or an operation. Suddenly hair seems so trivial.

****

I was wrong, partially, that is. Alberto did show up right after I decided to have another coffee, so the timing was perfect. And no word from Salvatore the *idraulico*, perhaps tomorrow—I will not hold my breath. Alberto and I got some nice projects checked off the list, well, project, at least. We cleared all the overgrowing plants away from the outside wall on the second *abbandonato*[107] terrace that was hanging over onto *via*

---

[107] *Abbandonato*. Abandoned

Casa Cinque[108]. It was just a matter of time before the *commune* (not "commune' as in the 70's, but *commune* as in Italian for "community") call the Marchese's to address and then it's a drama. And remember my motto for the year: No dramas! My girlfriend and faithful running companion, Monie, didn't think it would be possible. Of course, there is still one month to go. But so far, so good.

After taking care of clearing the wall, Alberto and I did an hour of leveling in the new "great *piazza*[109]" in preparation for the big gazebos that are to be delivered in the coming weeks. All plans are moving full speed ahead for the party Vivianna is putting on next June as well as Lui and Damiana's wedding the following September. After that, both Alberto and I think that it (the *piazza*) will make a most wonderful *orto* again—with nice gazebos to take shelter from the summer sun. I'm looking forward to it already. It's strange to think that they will be dining (in a nice gazebo) smack on the spot that my gigantic bonfire occupied last night. Sometimes things change at a glacial pace around here, sometimes not.

And we have new neighbors—just for a week—friends of Giuliana and Stefano named Varana, Raymond, and baby Luca—they come from Vienna. Rockets a bit confused by the baby backpack that Luca rides in on Raymond's back. New things disturb Rocket at first, and anything out of place. That's my dog.

Bello is in Milan today; he left yesterday and returns tomorrow— strategy meeting with the Milano office. And did he look good in his silver-grey, slightly shimmering, custom-made suit, paired with the perfect pin-stripped, dark blue (also custom) shirt with brown leather tennis shoes. He looks like he comes from the south of Italy. He pulls off the look nicely.

---

[108] *Via Casa Cinque*. Although named a "via" or passageway, via Casa Cinque – named after one of the original families of the village – comprises several flights of steep steps outside the eastern boundary wall of the villa.
[109] *Piazza*. Plaza.

Year 2 Living Abroad

9. July in Italia

Alas, it is almost the end of July and this is the first that I've sat down to write you—I will try and recall the best and worst of the month to share. I don't exactly know why I've been reluctant to write, or listen to music or get really excited about anything here at the villa for the past several weeks. It could be lingering effects from the passing of my favorite muse or the simple fact that spring is over and the summer, here, is simply a prelude to the fall—which reminds one of the coming winter.

Rocket

Rocket just bolted in from the great room— as he is never away from my side for more them five minutes. He has a little problem with separation. Actually, one could say he has a serious separation anxiety problem—but we are not into labeling. He is the epitome of the consummate good dog: great with kids, babies, all friends, strange dogs, eats his dinner when asked to, and listens to your commands. But God help a stranger who enters onto this property—which includes cats. Last night there was a furious commotion way up by the front gate that necessitated my investigating—Rocket had treed his nemesis kitty friend with whom he has been after all season. I figured it was about time, and good timing for us to leave the villa later this week for it is becoming very hot and it would have been a shame for all those chases to go without a little satisfaction in the end. It was the first time that my calls for him to come landed on deaf ears, but he is a teenager, and it was a cat.

The Cat Dog – Gallini

So much has taken place this month... I guess I'll start with things that you already know of... remember Mirella and Esteree—the two ladies that were staying in the *colombaia* for a month earlier this season? Mirella is the mother of this unknown Stefano (not Stefano Fittipaldi of

Stefano and Giuliana) who is a friend of Generoso's and has rented the *colombaia* (a one room box with crawl-in kitchen and closet bathroom where one can shower, shave, and sit on the commode all at the same time—by necessity). Well, after the *nonnas*[110] came and went and around the first of the month arrived the other brother (Enrico) with his wife (Rose), two young boys (Leonardo and Lorenzo), and their small greyhound (named *Gallini* or, as Bello refers to it: "Cat Dog"). An introduction was unscheduled and completely a surprise to me—well, not completely for *nana* had mentioned that her other son and his wife and two boys were coming later in the summer and we brushed it off as simply impossible taken the size of the *colombaia*. Well, shouldn't have. So, I am alone in the villa, one early July evening (Bello was in Milan) and I hear commotion at my door and Rocket barking, of course. Our front door, no easy task or common occurrence for you have to access to the green gate at the main walk—akin to busting into Fort Knox—or one must arrive from the street below, which has three gates to pass). We arrive up the landing to an unknown woman with two little boys talking at me in rapid Italian. I was completely perplexed. I kept asking where they were going and she kept saying that she didn't know and I would follow up with another question to try and qualify what was up and she kept saying that she didn't know—we were a collective mess. Finally, I followed her down the walk to ascertain just how they got onto the property, thinking that would help me determine where they were supposed to be headed. Well, that's when I met Enrico and Rocket met Gallini and promptly chased her off the side of the garden where she landed down at our abandoned terrace 20 feet below. It was like a moment out of an old Bugs Bunny cartoon where the Wile E. Coyote chases Bugs Bunny but Bugs pulls a fast move and leads the coyote over the cliff. It wasn't a good moment. I was barefooted, barely dressed and not in the mood to access the abandoned terrace (gated, locked, and totally overgrown with allergy-lased *erbacce*[111]) but did so immediately—while Rocket is running about barking and the kids are looking on traumatized. Poor Gallini. That was our first meeting.

---

[110] *Nonnas.* Italianglish for grandmothers
[111] *Erbacce.* Weeds

Subsequently, things have mellowed out. But Rocket loves to torture Cat Dog. Just the other day we were down at La Gavitella, the local "beach." Now the term "beach" is used loosely and vaguely here on the Coast and implies where the sea meets land. But don't be expecting a sandy beach, or even a trace of sand and it is here where everyone takes the sun, including our visiting family. Bello, Rocket, and I were going to take the new water taxi to Positano for a beach day where there is the nearest sand. Well, Rocket saw Gallini there and started toying with her by getting close to her family and getting her to chase him. At one point he had her in hot pursuit of him and right before he reached a boat on the landing he quickly changed directions to leave Gallini smacking her head and body on the beached boat—*he* thought it was very funny. Her family, however, did not. The family lasted all of three nights in the hot *colombaia* before I received a knock at our entrance by Enrico asking for help finding Generoso's hide-a-key. He had a desperate look on his face and said that they could not spend another moment in that *colombaia*. I warned his mother of this. Of course the brother never told the Marchese family that his mother and his brother (with the entire family) would each be coming for their own months at the villa before he took the place, so you can imagine how surprised everyone has been. They are a very nice family—though just a bit presumptuous. I can't wait to meet brother Stefano though—I want to ask him where he gets his gall.

✱✱✱✱✱✱✱✱✱✱✱✱✱✱✱✱✱✱

The boys from Agerola have returned to continue working on the Gagliano wall that fell down last year—sans mules, thankfully. Nice guys. I've never seen so much precision and effort go into the construction of a wall—perhaps it is because it is a redo. I've become friends with the entire Gagliano family—each separately though. And Rocket adores their dog Gregorio. We bought Grego a leash with the hopes of training him a bit when we take him for walks up in the mountains, but he prefers to be off leash—so be it. As I am sure you may recall, our first walk with Grego turned into a four-hour ordeal because he decided to follow some nice girls from Germany to

Montepertuso—the village perched above Positano. Of course we didn't know which way he went once he was out of sight, so we (Rocket and I) had to traverse the mountain back and forth giving everyone we could communicate with our phone number with the hopes of tracking him down. When we finally found Gregorio he was resting with the pack of German girls and he didn't feel like walking down the hill because by now it was high noon and very hot out. And by now I had also been carrying Rockettino for about two hours. It was a hellacious hike. But Grego is much better now. He still prefers to go off leash and when we start down the hill from a hike he prefers not to go home, but to take himself to La Gavitella for a swim. That's his business though. He was grounded for three weeks last time he did it and he is beginning to get it. Bello and I hiked with both dogs two weeks ago and we were accompanied by Nico Gagliano (fourth brother, 2nd, 3rd or 4th in line, I don't know) and, of course, Gregorio dashed ahead on the way down the hill. Nico was so mad. He said Grego would be grounded again if he went to the beach. We told him that he may as well just keep going down the hill to retrieve him and not to bother waiting for the call from the restaurant owner's down there. We were all wrong. We were no fewer then two steps from the Gagliano gate when Gregorio raced up from behind us and beat Nico to the gate. Score one for Gregorio. He didn't get grounded. And I've come to figure out exactly how all the balls that mysteriously appear on this property do so—and I am speaking of many balls—from tennis balls to soccer balls, new, Disney insignia balls to old stinky balls—and always in the garden...

Gregorio is a kleptomaniac. Seriously. I saw him in action up in the mountains at the *Convento San Domenico*[112] where he went into a neighboring yard and returned with a big fancy basketball-looking ball in his clutches. He wasn't to return it when I told him to do so. No, he kept it and hid it along the trail. The next time we were there he retrieved it and carried it further towards his house. He brings the balls down from his upper garden to the end of their garden and drops them down to

---

[112] *Convento San Domenico.* The convent and chapel perched 750 steps above the village.

ours with the hopes of me throwing it back to him. He most likes this game with oranges though, but this is not their season. He also plays catch with tomatoes. Subsequently, Rocket now likes tomatoes and loves oranges—he copies Gregorio. We are up to around seven balls for the season, thus far.

Maria Gagliano dropped me down some onions the other day that she had just pulled from the ground and I sent her up some fig jam from our garden. I will miss Maria this next season. We've begun to actually enjoy one another – not just in awe of... we still really can't converse in the conventional way – that's not so important though... and I really enjoy Giulio – he's a cool cat in my book. Oh – and Nicola isn't Brother No. 4, he's the first born... Some things just aren't as they seem... no, no... Or perhaps it's my Italian...

And talk about a small world—Alison (our dear friend and the one who runs my world while I'm here) was conversing with a Santa Barbara girl getting married in October. The bride-to-be was looking for a secondary reception location to celebrate with her local friends because she is getting married in Italy—in Cuore del Mare—in Montebello, actually. Her mother, Rachele, grew up here and is the cousin of Gennaro Gagliano (Maria's husband) and best friends with Angela (Luca's mom— where we shop for our groceries). She and I are now pen pals—she lives in Florida. She hasn't been back to Montebello since the birth of Luca 33 years ago. Both Angela and Maria were quite surprised when I told them the story. Unfortunately, we will not be here for the wedding, but it seems that Rachele's daughter wants to use our studio for her second reception. *Piccolo mondo*[113], indeed. Even from across the globe there are often just two degrees of separation.

And what about the dramas from last year, you may be asking? Not to ever be considered a foregone conclusion, I've made great inroads with having civilized relations with Irma and her kids. Luca (everyone is either *Luca* or *Gennaro* here—patron saints of the two churches in Cuore del Mare), Irma's husband, and I haven't made eye contact yet—next year

---

[113] *Piccolo mondo.* Small world

we will both be ready for that bridge. And Rocket doesn't try and bite their dog (*Briciola*[114], an appropriately named Chihuahua) anymore, although I've kept the two apart. All this male energy playing itself out. I will bring all the ladies below (Irma, her mom, her Aunt, her cousin Sylvia, and her parents [Maestro Domenico and Mrs. Maestro Domenico) all bottles of homemade marmalade before we leave. And I have a nice marmalade exchange going on with Mrs. Rispoli (another market) as well. If you've never tasted mandarin orange marmalade then you haven't fully lived—hers is to die for.

There was an incident though that took place last week between myself and Vivianna and it definitely rates as drama. Sorry Monie—I tried, really I did. Without getting into things too heavily, we disagreed on protocol and the decision-making hierarchy with regards to neighbors and relations and who can authorize who to do what. Let's just say I don't take kindly to being dictated to and that she doesn't take kindly to being rebutted. We'll work things out, next year.

Grumpy uncle and I have had a relatively quiet five months. Fortunately he never actually caught me picking oranges and lemons from the jointly shared, abandoned terraces—but he accused me of it. He's a grump, but not dumb. I, of course, didn't deny it. I skated by without a fig incident as well. I promised my girlfriend Monie that there would be no dramas this year. With regards to Grumpy uncle, I can say that held true.

Champagne is flowing and we are comfortably cruising at 35,000 feet. Dinner (early lunch for us) has been served and our steward and I have started to bond. Bello is busily completing the Times' *crossword puzzle and Rockettino is sleeping. I've just eaten some rather normal items, but ones that my body has not seen for almost half of the year, like lettuce and carrots (from points unknown) and duck and monkfish. I will pay for this later, guaranteed. Listening to '80s music on United's radio station and just enjoying the taste of champagne (as opposed to prosecco) and appreciating where we have been, what we have seen, and where we are going—there is much flying through my head.*

---

[114] *Briciola.* Crumb

Returning to the States is always a somewhat difficult transition for me, and one that becomes more difficult to reconcile each time it occurs. Sometimes I wonder if it is part of my impending (now present) midlife crisis taking shape, which is a luxury, I do realize. But for the record, it is my crisis, and no less real than others'.

Midlife... really?

Midlife is a funny place to arrive if you haven't arrived there yet or if one is still in denial. I like it, quite frankly. I got a fast taste of becoming different in the eyes of the youth when I shaved all my hair off. Going from long curls to a white head in course of 10 minutes without warning and monitoring the difference in how people (mainly strangers, mainly female) treat you is most interesting. It is like my lion's mane had been stripped and I was suddenly invisible. The Go-Gos playing now—"Our Lips are Sealed"—classic. Listening to "80s Revisited" while drinking French bubbles is definitely a way to fast-track oneself to a nostalgic ramble... (Wang Chung on now!) This is so apropos.

I could go on and on, however I think I will refrain. Back to the present... we just spent the past two days with Michael Phelps—well, kind of. He was staying at our hotel, as were the rest of the world swimming championship participants. Bello liked that and I kept thinking that I spotted Michael every time a tall person strolled by. I am pretty sure that I had an actual sighting right from our terrace, but that was during cocktail hour... And I love a hotel that welcomes dogs, has a Turkish bath and room service—and this hotel also had a rock-climbing wall that guests could try their skills on—it was a great experience—even in driving moccasins. They thought I was a bit nuts, at first.

Our co-pilot looks a little surprised that we are still standing after a few bottles of bubbles—I forewarned our crew of Bello's prowess, though— so they shouldn't be surprised but they always are, or seem to be. Brenda is our attendant. She's been on the job for 40 years and by the looks of her, you would think she were a liar. She just returned from Dubai with her children for a holiday. People are often not what they first seem.

Now, about the past month... it was a little odd, being there in July. As the season turned from spring to summer there was a sudden change in everything and everyone on the Costierra—and it wasn't for the better. I mean that with all sincerity and no prejudice. Before the solstice, there is an overwhelming sense of optimism in the garden as well as in the attitudes of the locals. After that full moon of the month of June, the energy changes. Suddenly, for the garden, the mode becomes about conservation and preparing for the impending warmer months, and the same attitude prevails among the locals on the coast—everyone and everything seems preoccupied with conserving their respective energies for the season of indifferent heat. I find that that oppressive heat takes no prisoners and either you adapt (flee, in our case) or perish. It is all a little dramatic for me, so it seems like the right time to go home.

Turbulence... Rocket hates this part of the Atlantic...

A Moment in Time
10.La Praia Moments (a Moment in Time with My Dog)

This has been one of those epic days that must be documented for future recollection... it has been that good. I'm sitting on my balcony overlooking La Praia[115], which is the local beach. La Praia is flanked by two huge cliffs that allow for a limited number of hours of sunlight and the entire village flocks here during the summer months. The scene is priceless and I will try and capture as much as possible... there are guys everywhere—fishing guys, hotel-owning guys, beach guys that sell tours and offer rides, and guys who seem to just hangout—but who knows on that one because as we've certainly learned on this trip: you never really know who you're seeing until you meet them here. At least that is how it is for me—I'm the new guy. And the new guy who kind of believes that any of these "guys" could actually give a damn. Fortunately, I have Rocket in tow to weaken the blow of the new guy on the other guys—who are definitely indeed all-guy kind of guys— regardless of their generation.

The ladies are fewer and far between. From what I've observed, the ladies of La Praia tend to be indoors (or at the corner of a patio) with a full sight of what all the guys are doing outside. Seems reasonable. The ladies run the show around here. Don't ask any of the guys to dispute that or you'll probably get hit.

Speaking about generations: three generations of whom I think are Italians just emerged from a far swim out in the October waters of La

---

[115] *La Praia*. *La Praia* is situated eastwardly around the point that separates Montebello from Cuore del Mare proper. Montebello is a "district" or "neighborhood" or "community" within the municipality of Cuore del Mare; the ridge that reaches to the point separates their two watersheds. La Praia is directly below Cuore del Mare, about 200 vertical feet below the road to Amalfi at the mouth of a narrow valley.

Praia and the youngest about 12 and the eldest about 70. Impressive, and…. A taxi just disgorged 10 tourists, who are scattering about faster than I can type, and the taxi has already turned around and headed back towards Positano… And *il patron*[116] can't seem to keep from looking up at my terrace and figure out whatever he's figuring out… he's fabulous and I haven't dared even approach him yet… he's obviously *A Alfonso Sr*[117]. He's tanned, utterly tasteful, and I venture to say that he has been proudly sporting his sideburns since the early '60s—no doubt, actually. You have to be a real "guy's guy" to be able to sport three different shades of purple in your attire (trousers, collared shirt and cashmere sweater—the "uniform" down here in South for well-heeled gentleman)—or, one who owns a large portion of something very valuable in your sphere of influence. Case in point here.

And speaking of the few females about… I ran into Gabriella—our girlfriend from Cuore del Mare who works at the shop *Kalima'* in Positano. Her *fidanzato*[118], Rafaele, runs their tour boat out of La Praia. She was here this morning when I emerged from my room's private staircase that leads right to the center of La Praia. La Praia is like a big living room (remember the cliffs) with balconies and everyone sits about watching everyone else—it's what Italians do in certain places. It is something like an opera that unfolds with the progressing hours of the day—starting with the first rumblings of the fishermen arriving around 5 am or to the beachgoers arriving for their day, the many boats coming and going (and all that that entails) and all set to the ever-constant and repetitive sound of the waves coming in and going against the gravel shore—you cannot escape that. But this opera is much better… Factor in the sounds of Italian guys yelling in some dialect only discernable by other Italians from the same specific area and the occasional child screaming, dogs barking, scooters scootering and buses

---

[116] *Il patron*. The boss.
[117] *A Alfonso Sr.* The patriarch of *Alfonso a Mare*. *Alfonso a Mare* ("Alfonso's by the Sea")—fronting the beach—is the name of the oldest, largest, and most established eatery, restaurant, hotel, and meeting point at La Praia. *Alfonso a Mare* houses the local chapel that serves this part of village.
[118] *Fidanzato*. Boyfriend, fiance

honking and have them all happen at once and that is this very second that I am experiencing here at La Praia— I would say it's the fourth or fifth act of the day and the next act of several more begin to unfold early evening at La Praia. After *la pausa*[119], of course.

Early evening for most Americans is the same as late afternoon for most Italians and, subsequently, most restaurants don't even open for another couple of hours—but believe me—*il patron* was the first to arrive to check out the catch of a couple of guys that had just come in— and *il patron* has a very severe limp and this is the farthest that I've seen him venture from his buildings—but anything for the best catch, I guess. He's headed off around the corner now towards La Africana (swank and crazy bar and disco set in two large caves above the water and with glass floors over the sea that was made famous in the '60s and '70s by the risqué habits of the long-time eccentric owner) and this may be my chance to meet him... oh no... he's back in the scene—checking out the offerings of yet another vessel—it would seem that Act 6 has begun... time for a glass of prosecco I guess—it being *aperitivi*[120] time and me being on the terrace and part of the scene—I should at least behave as such. Just a glass and not a bottle though—no need to be seen as an American foregone conclusion by any means—even if that includes hiding the bottle.

The first Americans have arrived for dinner (Act 7) and they are seemingly very confused as what to do because there is no staff in sight—heck, the lights aren't even on yet... in they go.... *il patron* is seated next to another older gentleman in purple—he must own something important nearby, too.

Almost 6 pm— still a little early for a respectable person to be having a drink—so, I'll refrain and stay in character. Someone acquiesced to the Americans and turned on the restaurant lights. Ada, the lady of the house (not far from the action ever), has now come into my view and

---

[119] La pausa. The afternoon pause, siesta
[120] *Aperitivi*. Cocktails and appetizers.

joined the stage. She made me a *doppio espresso macchiato*[121] per my request this morning AND augmented it with an additional pot of espresso and steamed milk. "Now *that* is really you knowing your guest," I told her. She must have caught me thinking about her because she is looking at me now... The ladies of La Praia catch everything.

---

[121] *Doppio espresso macchiato*. Double espresso with foam and a touch of steamed milk.

Book II: Year 3 Living Abroad (Excerpts)

11. Chapter 1. Loss and Rediscovery: The New Secret Garden

Spring Turns to Summer 2012: One Week First Season

June 6th. Day Two at Villa Montenelli – our new house – and today I ran to Amalfi. It is a really lovely run. Once you leave the village – and pass the *galleria*[122] and La Praia – it's a steady and hearty climb until one reaches Conca dei Marini – or so. Numerous kilometers. And the run downhill from there to Amalfi is a breeze – but then, there is the return…

June 7th. Day Three at the new *villa* (I used that term rather lightly here) and much has happened… as with everything in life, there are doors of opportunity that we either take or not—and the outcome of those choices define our each and every existence. So when we first saw the little rental house (with eat-in kitchen, laundry, and fabulous terrace) online and immediately noticed the same view as that of the Villa Marchese and il Frantoio, we knew we had to book it—so we did. That was about two weeks ago. It was a very good choice. The floors are all tiled and the walls freshly painted. The kitchen has a view from Positano to Capri with Li Galli and Balena[123] and the Sorrentine Peninsula[124] framing the entire scene: priceless. And come to find out this is the first year the place is being let for rental.

June 8th. Friday, Day Four at the villa… I snuck down to what I now call "the new garden" today and cleared a bit more—what I thought was a

---

[122] *Galleria*. Tunnel.

[123] *Balena*. Small, rocky island resembling a surfacing whale (*balena* = whale) situated beyond Li Galli and the Sorrentine Peninsula as one views Capri from the coast.

[124] Sorrentine Peninsula. The peninsula reaching from the mainland ending in Punta Campanella, which slopes seaward toward Capri. The peninsula forms a steep barrier between the villages on the Bay of Naples (including Sorrento) and those facing the Gulf of Salerno (including Positano and Amalfi).

gully is in actuality a staircase. I love undiscovered staircases about as much as anything else. So while I was down there snooping around in the brush and heading for this lovely last peach on the tree (what is it about lonely peaches on a tree past their prime that makes me want to trespass, I just don't know, but I find them entirely irresistible nonetheless) and just as I was about to reach it I noticed another person about 10 yards away—it immediately reminded me of similar covert scenes collecting citrus at the lower terraces at Villa Marchese with grumpy uncle patrolling in the distance, so I knew exactly what to do: duck and retreat... But that peach is mine...

****

I ran up to the cherry tree today—it was great to see her again and she saved a cherry in the exact spot where I found one last spring... she seemed to have grown in the past couple of years as her branches are higher and harder to reach... on the way down I had a vision of a friendly couple offering me a nice cold beverage (I was honestly thinking glass of white wine but that wouldn't be good for the coordination and the cliffs.... And no more than two minutes later I was passing Convento San Domenico and what happens—a charming young man comes from the chapel and offers me a cold beverage. I'm serious—and come to find out, Domenico's family owns the church property (or something like that) and he is doing the restoration work (or something like that) and he is there offering beverages (or something like that)—so who was I to say "no." He lives in Cuore del Mare and knows Claudia, so we will ask Claudia the story and not rely on my interpretation of things.

****

Last night we had drinks with Giulio at the Villa il Frantoio—the place looked good—like nothing had happened in 8 months... Just wrapping up lunch with Bello... he's already on today's *Herald-Tribune* crossword (they get more difficult as the week progresses, as you know) but I'm having a little piece of that beautiful ricotta that Signora Rispoli makes by hand... goes perfectly with the leftover tomato sauce that I made the other night and the leftover *cortecce*[125] pasta with *gamberetti*[126] that I mixed it with—perfectly (believe it or not).

Stefano and Giuliana arrive tomorrow... it will be great to connect. While I was passing the old Villa Marchese an hour ago while returning from my hike, it just so happened that Salvatore the gardener was leaving the villa at the very same moment and I got a chance to see my green gate open again—just as I had envisioned as I started my walk today... it was perfect timing—grace at work. The universe always provides and in this place it just seems to happen all the more often... Lunch was lovely and I think it is time for my nap. It really is so very civilized here in the most rugged of places.

Hoping to see Claudia this evening...

June 9th. Saturday, Day Four at the villa. Headed to Nerano[127] with Claudia and Bello and Raven[128] today—didn't know we were going to have a fourth but it was fun...

June 10th. Sunday, Day Five at the villa.... Today I'm heading up the hill to the sight of the old landslide... I think I'll take some photos and post them....

We had dinner at the villa last night with Generoso, Sandra, Alessandra (box set), and the new arrival Alvise of the *colombaia* and a nice photographer from Villa Giardino named Christian... it was great to be back. We're having dinner with Alvise tonight—just Bello and myself—everyone else has left...

June 12th. Monday, Day Six.

---

[125] *Cortecce*. Literally "bark" of a tree, a short and curled-shaped pasta that resembles a small canoe.
[126] *Gamberetti*. Shrimp
[127] *Nerano*. A beachside village – fishing port and popular excursion location for Italians – located between Positano and Punta Campanella. Easy to access by boat; long, arduous ride along steep, curvy, and narrow roads by car or bus.
[128] There could be an entire chapter or two on Raven...

I had Posiflora make a delivery today... the terrace is looking much better... all purples and blues and deep fuchsias that make the huge white planter boxes really pop... the neighborhood dog was having a fit seeing all of the sudden color in his view corridor—which means that everyone else noticed as well. Here, everything is noticed.

I walked down the hill early this morning with Bello to get the paper and some money for the plants and saw Tina and then Luca and later Mariella... it was great to see them all. Luca and I hung out at the bus stop and chatted for a while and then he had me for a *caffè*[129]—it was really nice. Of course I ran into Signora Rispoli and had forgotten my present for her... she said she had a little something for me and not to worry and we would see each other later—which could be another year or two and she and I will have not skipped a beat.... Then it was time that I went over to see Giulio at the fish market.

On the way up the hill I ran into Maestro Domenico today and asked him if he had seen the new and improved *colombaia* care of Alvise's tasteful refinishing. He hadn't... then I saw Alvise from his tower. Last night was pretty lovely for us all.

---

[129] Caffè. Coffee

Book II: Year 3 Living Abroad, Chapter 2

12. Chapter 2. Spring and Summer at the New Villa

Monday, May 13th.

I've just returned from a five-hour walk. And I didn't really go all that far. That's easy to do here—walk and spend hours and actually really go not that far—but do not get that confused with not seeing or doing that *much...* quite the contrary... The day started off at 6:00 *in mattina*[130] to an incredibly loud roar of thunder in the not-so-far distance and I knew we were in for a wet early morning drama. (Here, everything is a drama—either in the literal sense of the word or just the essence of everything being dramatic in its nature—I guess that they are the same thing in actuality.) But the springtime rains are very fleeting in their nature, so we decided to take a nice walk while my gardening shoes, which I had mistakenly left out the evening prior, had a chance to dry out.

So, off Rocket and I went—ascending our stairs and presented with the first option of many: which way? *Sinistra o destra?* right? We opted to head up the hill, toward Cuore del Mare proper and the little church at the top of the hill that I love so much. The walk to the little church can be done in less than 10 minutes if one walks in earnest—but this morning wasn't that kind of morning and the stroll was prolonged threefold. Along the way, Rocket met Lucky (a two-year-old white little character attached to a very nice local woman). It was all about the dogs, so proper introductions were skipped until next time around— what's the hurry, right?—nobody is really going anywhere anytime soon. After a few minutes of our mutual admiration of our sidekicks, I return to my exaggerated slow stroll and off Lucky and his counterpart went—continuing their very busy morning, too.

---

[130] *In mattina.* In the morning.

It wasn't long until I reached the church and decided to continue on to the top of Cuore del Mare when I heard and spotted a lovely *Praianese* couple walking gingerly down the steep road, seemingly arguing in a strong *Praianese* dialect, but which I understand fully as simply speaking. (*Praianese* dialect is much like *Napolitano* dialect: unique to their specific region and generally impossible for the outsider's ear to grasp.) And then her attention turned to me!

"Here we go… I'm not going to understand a word of this," I thought. But to much my surprise, I was able to basically make out that there was rain coming on the horizon and that I had better get to wherever I was going. So out of respect for my fellow *Praianese*, I agreed and thanked her and abruptly started down the hill, back toward the little church where I hear my name being called from a familiar voice. It was Luca (one of a dozen we know, I assure you.) This Luca is a friend of Claudia and a nice guy in general. He had just completed his *giro*[131] to the village and was headed home, so I decided to follow along and have a little visit. As we strolled the 40-some yards to his turn along the *via*[132], we ran across several ladies Luca knew and brief salutations were exchanged and a smile of somewhat recognition given to me—as Cuore del Mare proper really isn't my neighborhood and there isn't much call to really know those that don't live directly in your neighborhood, but the acknowledgement felt nice. (And everyone loves Rocket!)

Being that I was now directly in the area of our girlfriend Claudia's house, I decided to give her a yell from the road to her balcony, but to no avail—so I stopped in at Gennaro's shop instead—I never miss an opportunity to stop in at Gennaro's (nephew of Angela Fusco who we shop with regularly and the mother of another Luca who delivers our groceries and owns the gym that Bello frequents daily) and have a look around. Gennaro sells everything for the house that isn't edible. From water hoses to bathmats, glass canning jars to batteries… and gardening implements! I just love his shop. I took my position in the nonexistent

---

[131] *Giro*. Literally "a turn" or "a round" – commonly used to mean "visit" or "short trip."
[132] *Via*. Path, passageway.

118

queue so I could ask Gennaro about some gloves and by the time the shop calmed down to a low roar I had assembled an arm full of interested *cose*[133]: A sickle for cutting weeds (almost scary and illegal looking), a pair of the best gardening gloves in the house (which I will undoubtedly destroy after no more than 12 consecutive hours of work), three lovely marmalade vases, and a replacement blade for one of my previously purchased saws. In the chaos, Gennaro (in full Italian) introduces me to two gentlemen that he thought could possibly help me with my garden clearing—as I had briefly asked him in passing three days prior (at the suggestion of his aunt) to please keep an eye out for me—good thing I showed up when I did today. So, after about 10 minutes of explaining where my house and garden are amongst the entire store, it was decided that Antonio and Bastiano would come by tomorrow and take a look. Whew—that felt good to me.

At checkout time I realized that I had very little money with me as I was originally simply going out for a walk, so I asked Gennaro if I could come back later and settle up—that's one of the beautiful aspects of this place—he, of course, said "no problem, Giacomo" and off I went with my bag of goodies thinking I would simply go home but realizing I had still yet to pick up the paper and knowing that I may not leave the house again for days, I took a right turn and headed towards the village— although all turns ultimately lead to the same place☺ Along the way I ran into an acquaintance of ours named Rosa and we exchanged kisses and caught up on her world and ours and off she went.

I decided to stop in over at Villa Frantoio to see if my buddy Giulio was in and perhaps have a visit and a *caffè*, as I had now been out for three hours. Of course Giulio was in and spotted me upon entering the gate— he was up in a persimmon tree trimming. We hung out at his new pool and placed the blue sun sails that I brought from America and decided to donate to him—as they didn't really work with my terrace motif of plain and empty--borderline austere—a little too "American *au courant*" for my tastes here, I tend to go for the more *rustico*[134] feel with my

---

[133] *Cose.* Things
[134] Rustico. Rustic

furnishings. I guess the grass is always greener somewhere else. After our visit and my *caffè* and being right next door to the old villa, I couldn't help but decide to go and check it out and see what was up...

So Rocket and I hopped over and down the wall and went for a very special walk as I really wanted to place some flowers on Jackie Chan's gravesite in the main garden. And I did. It felt really good. It was a little sad walking the grounds though—the place looks like crap. Sad really. But that's a different story all together. I did pick some extra roses and decided that after my stroll of the grounds I would go get my newspaper before the *giornale*[135] shop closed at 1:00 and bring a bouquet to Angela for Mother's Day.

No sooner had I left the grounds of the villa that I ran into Pietro returning from the village with bags of provisions. He's living almost full time at the villa now—fortunately he didn't notice or seem to care about the roses brimming from my bag and I played dumb to the fact that he has two cats living with him at the villa as I had already spotted their bowls of food and such during my snoop about. I invited Pietro over for a drink this week—it's always more fun to drink with someone. He agreed and off he went. I made it to the *giornale* just in time before closing and retrieved my precious *International Herald-Tribune*, the only real newspaper as far as I'm concerned. (The *Herald-Tribune* is the international edition of the *New York Times* printed in London a full day ahead of American news and about four days ahead of American newspapers—it's very cosmopolitan and globally inclusive and the only lifeline I have beyond the confines of the coast).

Feeling like I had accomplished all that I had set out to do this morning and more, I proudly strolled the 100 yards down the street to Angela's market and gave her her flowers. She was very touched. I picked up a little *pane*[136] and Rocket lead the way back up toward our house, as he was tired and wanted to be home to take a nap—I can tell these things. But, in typical costierra fashion, we weren't quite finished yet. Again, I

---

[135] Giornale. Newspaper, journal
[136] *Pane.* Bread

hear my name... "Giacomo!"... and then a scooter pulls up. It is Bastiano, the gardener. He confirms, yet again, my location up the street (its only one of the oldest and best positioned gardens in town and has the reputation of its being abandoned for 30 years—so it's not that hard to find) and we changed plans for tomorrow's meeting time to today at 5.00 o'clock—at least I think that's what we agreed to—again, Cuore del Mare dialect is a little hard to fully grasp....

So, there you have it. In two hours I think I have an appointment—I'll let you know. In the meantime it is time for a glass of Pinot Grigio and a garden walk... it being 3:00 o'clock and all. Actually, I'm a bit tardy.

It's now 6:00 pm and Bastiano, in his apparent resilience, showed up to tour the grounds promptly at 5:00—and in the pouring rain. So, I thought: Why not...? He started off with pointing out to me that my simple laurel hedge at the entry gate needed trimming a bit (I had just taken care of it the week prior to both my neighbors and my specific liking) but I, very gently, assured him that that was the very least of our possible concerns and to please follow me to the "garden," more akin to an overgrown and abandoned forest, you see... but the villa has a past and our section of the villa (in most glorious of days) was reserved for the livestock. Interesting, no? But back in the day, this family – this Napolitano family – had working (a *real* working) villa, the kind we only hear about but I was told of... and I became a man on a mission...

Now, in the interim, you may have surmised that I had a nice two hours' break from my trying existence and was in repose with my Pinot Grigio in hand and Rocket in tow—and you would be close—but not exact. Just as I poured my glass and closed my laptop I heard the gate bell ring—I loathe that sound—much like my doorbell in Santa Barbara, which is disconnected. I really don't like surprises in general. I reluctantly buzzed the gate open without knowing who was there and thinking that I had to receive whoever it was regardless so, why not just go for it with pleasure... and it was Donato...

Donato is this random (at the time) person who stopped me on the beach in Positano four days prior to engage me in his pure fascination that he had with Rocket and how Rocket reminded him of their dog from a few years past—a really nice guy. But this was his third of such determined encounters within the previous three hours and, quite frankly, both Rocket and I were getting use to it and, as always, happy and appreciative to respond with appropriate retort. So we had a nice visit and off he went to find his wife. Now, rewind to yesterday afternoon when Rockettino and I are walking Mariella up the street and helping her with her groceries while lobbying her for her help here at the house with the terrace and things while we are not here. (Mariella, her sister Tina, their mother, Maria, and I go back 15 years and they live directly above us by about 100 yards—Tina used to work for Generoso at the Marchese Villa cleaning his house and Maria and Lady Marchese are contemporaries—but of vastly different universes. I love Maria—she makes the strongest coffee and you want to be careful when you leave the room with her, for she always has something to say, *sempre*[137]! She's classic.) Well, I no sooner turn around to head down to our house and there's Donato for the second time raving about Rocket and his perfect behavior. And then come to find out that he is staying at the bed and breakfast right below Maria's house and up above our place above the street... *piccolo mondo*[138], indeed. We chatted and I invited him over (I tend to do that) and, hence, the visitor at our gate...

(There is something that I find quite refreshing and very civilized about being buzzed in at a gate and asked questions later—like a welcomed and expected guest. (Alicia taught me that one. So, I try to follow suit— and hope for the best☺)

... I welcomed Donato with little surprise but much more interest and genuine pleasure—like I said: he's a really nice fellow. We greeted and he made sure that my open invitation from the day prior was just that— open, and timely. I assured him it was both by pouring him a glass of *vino bianco*[139] and offered to tour the house and invited him for a walk in the garden. He was game and off we went. He got the B-ticket tour due to the fact that he and his wife, Giovanna, were going to go to

---

[137] *Sempre*. Always.
[138] *Piccolo mondo*. Small world.
[139] *Vino bianco*. White wine.

Positano for the evening—but he wound up being a bit late for, apparently, Donato is a garden buff, too. We toured the garden grounds had a nice visit while discussing the possibility of his renting our place for a month next year. (I love nothing more then quick-fire introductions AND negotiations—regardless of the topic—it's just so, lively.) He seemed to know what he wanted to talk about prior to arriving—he refrained from small talk and got right to his desired topic of conversation. I really respect that. (Foreplay is for lovers and not business dealings in my book.)

Well, that was exactly one week ago. Much has happened and most of it predicted last week—just not in the exact timeframe that I was envisioning. I guess that's just life. Bastiano was a no show for the later days of last week due to either another job or the sheer scope of this one. In either case, Franco had been a godsend. He's so cool, from Naples—he knows his gardens and we've bonded beautifully. We both speak limited second languages—but we more than manage. And the sheer amount of brute force that Franco exhibits, while possessing a certain degree of finesse, is hard to replicate.

July 15th. 30,000 feet above the Alps – Bello has by now made it back to the Costierra with Rocket. I hope that my boy is doing all right... and I returning back home briefly to tend to a very important event. I don't know if surreal even begins to describe what I am experiencing at this very moment. I'm the sole passenger in the First Class cabin of a Lufthansa 747-8 (the "-8" makes it the absolute newest in the fleet). Alone. The sole passenger. The caviar cart was dedicated solely to my pleasure. I absolutely enjoyed every minute and made sure that ample made its way back to the crew... but a half pound of sevruga goes a long way.... I have moved over to my "writing cubicle" being that I have six seats to select from throughout my flight. My sleeping chamber has been set up for the past two hours already and I've delayed dinner for another hour so I may chat with you and go for a tour upstairs and find someone to talk to. I'll be right back....

My personal bathroom has its own window and seating area…. This is beyond civilized and I think I have to really absorb this for a few moments….

Lola is taking excellent care of me and the flight's purser made a point of intruding himself to me and briefly took a moment to properly connect…

Best night's sleep ever on a plane… 450 thread-count, minimum…

Back to 30,000 feet, but now over the Midwest. We really do have a most beautiful county to fly over. Lola woke me a while back and gently asked me just how I prefer my eggs. Seriously. I thought that I would keep things simple and requested an omelet…

Already missing the coast.

Back in Italia

Around July 24th. I'm spending the day in solitude. It's nice. I know this is going to sound awfully trite and perhaps a cliché of many sorts, but I just returned from a garden walk with a *bellini*[140] and clippers and gathered a perfect bunch of wild foliage as a memory bouquet photo I'll send to Caterina and then bring to Giuliana as a hostess thought tonight at dinner, but all the while singing aloud to Andrea Bocelli with my earphones in. I never paused to listen to how I sounded, but I'm sure it wasn't so good.

The garden is looking wonderful as the olive trees and the incredible old walls are all fully exposed to the sun and wind and they radiate an energy that almost shines—yes, even the stone walls are being expressive. Franco has been just about as perfect a new friend and property caretaker one could imagine, but I tend to be so consistently fortunate in the individuals that opt to work with me—I'm really the lucky one in all instances, so I try to do my best. It keeps you on your toes: Gratitude.

---

[140] *Bellini*. Cocktail of prosecco and peach juice.

Over at the Villa Marchese

Tina from Brunico is visiting with Stefano and Giuliana all week, perfect timing. And Catherine, part of the Norwegian mafia, is here for two weeks—imperfect timing for Giulio... Mia Mia (his current girlfriend) isn't so thrilled and she sticking to him like glue. Understandably so from a woman's point of view, I suppose. Please, someone tell me.

What a three-week period that was...

I just returned with dinner to go from La Strada and although I haven't been in town for the past month or so and I showed up unannounced, I was greeted with smiles and *baci*[141] from everyone. *Il patron*[142] was out front and gave me a strong handshake and Daniela was close by with her big *baci* and a glass of prosecco. I said hello to the guys in the kitchen and placed my order to take away for tonight as I choose to dine *in casa*[143].... While dinner was being prepared, I ventured up to the terrace where Nicolo and cousin Lorenzo were pleasantly surprised by my visit and stopped for a moment from their busy night to say hello— and then I spotted Silvia, and she toured me around their improved *al fresco*[144] terrace... the entire experience is like returning to your cousins' kitchen for a warm reception and great meal—but it is the company that makes the experience—as it typically is.

I'll let you know how dinner was in an hour or so...

---

[141] *Baci.* Kisses
[142] *Il patron.* The boss
[143] *In casa.* At home
[144] *Al fresco.* Open air

Book II: Year 3 Living Abroad, Chapter 3

13. Chapter 3. Autumn, Back at the Garden...

Ciao ciao, bello or bella of mine.

I'm back at home... our other home – Italia (sans Bello though—he's in Tunisia today). But it feels so good. It's Sunday afternoon and the village is as quiet as imaginable. The rain is subtle but the change of season is apparent. Just two hours ago, I was in the garden doing what pleases me most and finding it necessary to shed a top layer of clothing, but things can change quickly around here this time of year. Now I am showered and in my new matching thermo undergarments, enjoying a glass of Pinot Grigio while listening to '80s music and writing to you... Rocket is napping and ABBA never sounded so good... "The Winner Takes It All".... It's a really sweet song... kind of sad, but just a little... now a little Eros Ramazotti.

.... Leftover pasta from last night with a little prosciutto added today is warmed up in the *forno*[145] and I think I will elaborate on the past few days before lunch and then a nice nap... Now a little Ottmar Liebert (Diondra, here's to you)...

Where do I start... sometimes the beginning isn't the place... hmmm. Right now feels pretty lovely. Sometimes it's difficult to find real happiness with the moment and today I'm not allowing that to happen. I'm just being honest here. And its not that I'm a depressive kind of guy—you know that. But I am going to lighten up a bit. (It seems appropriate.)

I want to share this space with so many of your for so many very different reasons for you—all the same for me... to see you enjoy

---

[145] *Forno.* Oven

yourself. Also, to share with you what makes me really happiest. (Now on to 1999 Salvation Live by Pascual Feat—on Hotel Costes #2. Check it out.)

So, yesterday, Giovanna and Rocket and I went for a great and pleasantly predictable hike up the path of the Gods... it rained on us and we had the best little picnic lunch up at my old cherry tree.

... Days later and it's a mixed rainy and sunny day... I'm taking the opportunity to actually sit and write you before the moment flees... "Mai Piu Cosi' Lontano" by Bocelli lilting off my MacBook plays...

After Giovanna left for her *giro*[146] to the Apulia coast, I settled in and have been going nonstop it seems. Franco has been here two full days and will return tomorrow. The garden looks better and better each day and it wasn't such a *casino*[147] upon my arrival... Janis Ian... "At Seventeen"... I love these moments... I think it is time for a short glass of Angela's new house *vino*[148]—it's really good and more economical and a bigger bottle—what's not to like? (I am conserving the empty bottles and their special corks for next year's olive production and to pass out as gifts... I'll get back to you on that...

Speaking of olives—the olive grove is an orchard once again (once the burn piles are processed) and we've begun trimming the actual olive trees themselves—each one based on its shape and personality. After a year and a half I feel as if I know them a bit and deserve the privilege of the task. The entire experience is just that—a huge privilege. Franco planted a winter vegetable garden as a present to me.

There's a funny incident that happened with me at 5:00 *in mattina una settimana fa*[149] that I have to share... it has to do with a trespassing hunter and his shot gun and my kicked-in gate and the barking neighbor

---

[146] *Giro.* Trip, excursion
[147] *Casino.* Mess, chaos
[148] *Vino.* Wine
[149] *In mattina una settimana fa.* In the morning a week ago

dog and my catching him and confronting him and the ensuing chase through my neighbors' garden...

It all started God knows when—when those who chose to *come here and hunt* began, I suppose. It started for me upon my first foray into the forest garden and I seemed to be surrounded by discharged bullet casings... I think that's what there are called in English—*caducci*[150] here. Fast forward to last week and the discovery by Franco of new, ultra fresh casings of less than 36 hours old... (they know these things here). I, of course, was seriously disturbed by the matter as one casing was found at the end of our terrace area at our big fig tree—way too close for comfort. I was determined to set up camp in the upper olive grove where we found the bulk of the new shells (not so cleverly stashed behind a rock when a pocket would have done so much better).

Franco assured me that morning was the ideal time for dove hunting (how silly) and I shouldn't be worried.... I took his advice and went to bed early— determined to catch in the act whoever this was. And *in fatto*[151]—that's exactly what happened.... When you go to bed at 8:00 p.m., 5:00 a.m. feels like a pretty reasonable time to be stirring, and that's exactly what I was doing that morning... and then I heard the neighboring dog bark a few times and it took possibly a few moments for me to realize that I was awake and why that was and then another bark and suddenly I'm putting two and two together and I'm up out of bed and getting dressed. (I suggest one going to bed clothed when on stakeout.)

So, I rush out on to the terrace and I am very quiet and still and Rocket follows suit... then I see the grass reeds below moving in deliberate manner and then I see nothing and a few moments later a see a figure moving through my new vegetable garden and I immediately yell out for him to stop and identify himself—all in very assertive and clear English—he got the point ☺ and then Rocket went off in dog language— which is pretty international. He ran down deeper into our garden and I

---

[150] *Caducci.* Part metal, part plastic discharged bullet casings which tend to litter preferred shooting locations.
[151] In fact.

ran back into the house to find my shoes and my dog—who was already deep in hot pursuit. I was petrified that Rocket would get shot and had awful visions as I ran from room to room looking for my bloody shoes. Rocket returns quickly and we race to the upper garden to see if any of my twig traps had been passed through and we determine that "he" is still down in the garden somewhere and we race back towards terrace for the best vantage point and in closest proximity to my coffee machine to wait him out... I know this whole story is rather predictable but that's the funny part... I couldn't make up this stuff... so, after a few minutes of perching, I spot this lone figure peering from atop the lowest terrace on the property and, again, I demand to know who he is and why he's there—this time in quasi Italian. He seems pretty normal and even though he was carrying a shotgun (which you just don't see here everyday), it seemed reasonable at the time to approach. We met—I was visibly upset and snapped a photo of him and off he ran into the neighboring garden—a garden he knew far too well to be his first time.

I decided to follow suit and on to the neighboring rooftops is where he retreated and where we lost him. I don't think he will be back anytime soon though. I can be a bit much to take, especially at 5.00 a.m.

Printed in Great Britain
by Amazon

39114088R00079